Retirement is Just the
BEGINNING

The Union Worker's Guide to Dealing with a Retirement Strategy

Daniel J. DeVerna

Norsemen Books

Print edition ISBN: 978-1-988172-33-0

Printed in the United States of America
Published by Norsemen Books

www.dandeverna.com

*Daniel J. DeVerna, Investment Advisor Representative.
Securities and investment advisory services offered solely
through Ameritas Investment Corp. (AIC). Member FINRA/
SIPC. AIC and Creative Financial Partners are not affiliated.
Additional products and services may be available through
Daniel J. DeVerna or Creative Financial Partners that are not
offered by AIC.*

Norsemen Books

AUTHOR'S NOTE

The reason I wanted to write this book is because I grew up in a Union family and carried on the tradition before I became a financial consultant. My Dad worked for Barry Equipment in Perrysburg, Ohio and the memory of him going on strike has resonated with me for my entire life. It had a direct impact on my family that I was aware of then, and am especially aware of now. My Dad would eventually leave that company and start a welding business, but the mentality of workers' rights and the backbone of those that are protected by Unions stuck with him and was imparted upon me.

When I became an adult, I began working for Cooper Tire and we were a Union shop. Since I had already grown up in a Union household, I was quite comfortable working in this situation. In fact, I saw the many benefits first hand and I knew personally how things like labor disputes could have an effect on the lives of real families. Families just like my own. For instance while I worked at Cooper Tire I saw the Union workers gain the upper hand in contract negotiations with management and realized how working for a Union shop could have many advantages. With that said, I've seen how circumstances can later turn negative on you. That same factory later on saw those same jobs leave for Kentucky and Mexico and now no longer exists. That seems to me to be an example of how life can change on you, even when you think you are protected. To me, and I hope that you will see this once you have read this book, the necessity of preparing for difficult times is of the utmost importance.

Whether you read this book and end up a client of mine, already are one, or take the information that follows and are able to better serve your needs on your own, I will feel as though, this book was a success.

CONTENTS

ENDURANCE

It was suggested to me to start this book off with a story about survival which in turn would lead to the illustration of life lessons about preparation and planning. This parable would set up the book and its theme for the chapters that follow. The moral to the story would really hammer home to you, the reader, the lessons in why you should use a financial consultant and why planning and saving for retirement are so paramount.

So I read stories about survival. Stories of brave men who faced the cruelest of the elements and circumstances. Stories of defying crushing odds and living to tell the tale. These stories were indeed inspiring. One in particular stood out for the purposes of this book. The true tale of Antarctic explorer Ernest Shackleton and his fateful voyage aboard his ship, Endurance. A voyage on which his crew and he were trapped by sea ice, a crushing cold that would nearly claim the lives of his entire crew.

But the real link from that story to this story is the name of his vessel. Endurance. Because if I have learned anything about life, it is that you need endurance. For the race of life, as the saying goes, is a marathon not a sprint. You have to be prepared for unexpected things along the way so that your survival is never in jeopardy. You have to plan for being in the race all the way to the finish line.

The suggestion of how I would begin this book included linking the moral from the survival story to the necessity for a leader on your own financial survival voyage—a ship's captain if you will. And it was suggest that I be thought of as that leader, that captain. But here is the truth of the matter. No one. Let me repeat, no one, not even me, cares more about your money than you do. The truth is this. You are the leader, the captain of the ship, on your personal financial voyage. My role is that of the navigator and pilot. You tell me where you want to go, and I will chart the course to help get you there. So with that said, let the journey begin!

In the book *Fantastic Voyage: Live Long Enough to Live Forever,* authors Ray Kurzweil and Terry Grossman talk about the possibilities of extending life through the exponential advances that are taking place in the field of medicine. They explain that if you can take care of yourself, sooner or later scientific breakthroughs would happen. The possibility of outlasting death, to live to an age once thought inconceivable, could be a reality.

Even if you don't completely buy into that notion, or maybe don't even want to live "forever", you do need to consider that you will probably live much longer than your parents and ancestors. This is important because it can help determine your needs for a happy and productive retirement. It is just a simple fact of life that your retirement needs must factor a longer lifespan into the equation.

As an example, I have breakfast with my 93-year-old Grandfather every week. He drives himself in his Mercury Grand Marquis to meet me. He is of sound mind and is still enjoying his life. The funny part to his personal retirement story is that he has been retired from BP/SOHIO for longer than the 33 years that he worked there. Oh, I should mention that he did have a small break in his career at BP/SOHIO. Like most fellows of his generation, he took time out to go and fight in a little thing called World War II before returning home to work.

Can you imagine what problems he'd be faced with to-day if he didn't have a retirement plan in place? I think that his example illustrates why I get so much gratification from helping people like you prepare for what should be the best years of your life.

Let's do some more imagining for a minute. Imagine that you live a healthy and lengthy life beyond your working years. Imagine that you have dreams that remain unrealized. Maybe a bucket list of travel locations and accomplishments yet to be fulfilled. Perhaps you have children and grandchildren that you wish to help on their paths to the best lives possible. These wonderful things along with some less than pleasant possibilities like injuries, illnesses, and medical care for your spouse or yourself are exactly the reason that I am writing this book. Because I love my job as a financial consultant and I care about my clients. To be honest, and I admit a little bit of selfishness here, I feel so rewarded and have an overwhelming sense of accomplishment in helping my clients achieve their retirement goals.

You also may have plans prior to retirement that require action and forward thinking so that those goals can be realized without burden. Things like buying a vacation home, taking the trip of a lifetime, or helping with college tuition for children and grandchildren takes planning. And sound planning can take the worry out of your daily thoughts and let you focus on the present moments. After all, isn't that what life is supposed to be about? Enjoying the now, capturing the essence of life as it unfolds. My job is to make this easier for you.

Throughout this book, I'll explain some of the how's and why's of financial planning. I will also tell you some personal things about my own path that I hope will help earn your trust.

Because let's face it, you work hard for your money and you shouldn't let just anybody manage it. After all, it's your future that is at stake. So whether it is me or someone else looking after your investments, you better be able to trust them. My wife makes fun of me, but I tell my clients, that you had better get the warm fuzzy from your financial consultant. I think you know what I am talking about when I say that. I am also and most importantly speaking to competence. Obviously, I can't give away all of my secrets in this short of a book, but I will help you to understand how and why I go the extra mile to ensure that my clients, no matter the size of their portfolio, have the potential to benefit from the available investment platforms that are best suited to their portfolio. This is in part accomplished by my drive to both understand and stay ahead of the changing conditions that influence the market. Things like politics, innovation, and the evolution of consumer's needs. I do this so that you don't have to. I worry and prepare and plan so that you can spend more time on your purpose.

Do I sound important? Well let me knock myself down a few pegs. I'm only valuable to you if I get you the results that give you that warm fuzzy. Whereas if your car breaks down on the side of the highway, the most important person you know will be your mechanic. I mention this to keep things in perspective. Financial planning is important, but so are a lot of other things.

Now you may be saying to yourself, I should have gotten on board this train a long time ago. Now might be a little too late to get started. Well for those of you late bloomers who feel this way let me tell you about an ancient Chinese proverb that still makes a lot of sense. It goes like this:

> *The best time to plant a tree is 20 years ago,*
> *the second best time is now.*

No matter what rung of time's ladder you are on, it is never too late to plan for your future.

So who am I? Well I'm Daniel J. DeVerna, financial consultant with Ameritas Investment Corp., member FINRA/SIPC. The truth is I'm a husband, proud father of four children, good friend, and a regular guy who happens to take a lot of pride in his work and feels like he is pretty good at it.

I wasn't always a financial consultant. In fact my roots are as small town and blue collar as you can get. My parents were hardworking, God fearing, country folks who did not make a ton of money, but kept my family fed and clothed and taught me the value of honest work. They instilled in me the drive to succeed. This drive has been further propelled by life itself. I had my first son very young and in short order became a single Dad. For a twenty year old, who wasn't that far from being a kid himself, it was a lot of pressure. I had no choice but to grow up in a hurry.

I worked making tires on the graveyard shift at Cooper Tire. It was honest, hard work, and frankly, I made pretty darn good money doing it. But I wanted something else. So while still working the graveyard shift I started working as a financial consultant. I was burning the candle at both ends and in the middle, don't forget, I had a baby at home. To be honest, in those first months I wasn't finding any success. I considered giving up. I wrote on my whiteboard in my office these words: President's Club or Garbage Man. What I meant was, that if I didn't make that year's upcoming President's Club I would resign myself to work at Cooper tire forever.

I went to work with a new attitude. The attitude that I was going to be the best financial consultant that my company had. That year I made the President's Club. I devoted my life to my family and I purposed myself to helping others with their financial goals. I've done this ever since with one quality that I take to work every day. Intensity. The people that know me know that that's probably the one word that best describes my work ethic. Whether it's my intensity to be at the top of the business of financial consultancy, or the intensity I take to the dojo where I've practiced martial arts for the past ten years. I even have the Japanese character for the word intensity tattooed on my chest. I literally take it everywhere with me.

Nowadays I have over 700 households that count on me for their financial consulting. And I've got to tell you, it is both a source of pride and an obligation that I take very seriously. Besides my family, it is the single biggest factor that drives me every day to better myself. Those 700 plus households continually motivate me to grow as a person.

Multiple times a year I reinvest in myself for the purpose of serving my client's needs in the most productive and beneficial ways possible. In fact, I reinvest in myself through quite a few means, on a weekly basis, partly driven by that aforementioned intensity that I have, but mostly so that I never allow myself to become complacent or comfortable. I meet personally with my clients on a regular basis whether in my office or by traveling to them, sometimes clear across the country.

I still believe in looking someone in the eye and shaking their hand. In this world of instant and impersonal communication I try to keep alive the old fashioned values that my parents' and grandparents' generations believed in so much. And I count my blessings and attribute much of my own success to this way of conducting business. My guess is that you will appreciate it also.

So let's continue now with some examples of the most common questions that I have gotten in my many years as a financial consultant. I will expound on these in the chapters that follow in more detail, but for now here is a glimpse at what you can expect. You probably have already thought of most of these questions. But regardless, my purpose for this book is to help you understand the value in having a person like me work for you. As I mentioned earlier, you have worked hard for your money and no one cares more about it than you. But dealing with the intricacies of managing it is probably not your purpose in life, what fulfills you, or frankly how you want to spend your time. It is, however, my purpose. So let me see if I can get you the warm fuzzy. Here goes:

1. WHEN CAN I AFFORD TO RETIRE?

This is a question I get a lot. And the answer for union workers is even more perplexing. Factors like multiple and complicated retirement plans, social security questions, and budgetary issues among employers muddy the already seemingly unclear waters.

The very decision to retire can be a source of stress because of the emotions that it brings up. The thought of leaving a work environment that has been such an important part of your life, as well as the colleagues and friends that you have spent so much time with, can be difficult.

Later in the book I will get into the nitty gritty of the details and cover all the bases. I will discuss things like how your age, financial circumstances, health, and family situation affects the decisions you will make. I will also talk about the timing of eligibility of collecting retirement benefits from your pension(s) or other sponsored retirement plans. We'll also examine some of the biggest factors involved in answering this question. Like, what kind of lifestyle would you like to have in retirement? Where would you like to retire? How long will your retirement last?

I'll try to keep your interest while answering these and other very serious questions and hopefully we might even have a little fun with it. After all, isn't retirement supposed to be fun? In my book, it is!

2. HOW WILL I PAY FOR HEALTH CARE IN RETIREMENT?

If you follow the news at all you know that health care is a hot topic. Health care seems to be ever changing. All the rhetoric about changing the health care laws and entitlements can be scary. Pharmaceutical companies seem to pull the prices for drugs randomly out of a hat, and the costs just seem to increase. The same can be said about most other elements of the health care system. It is convoluted to say the least, elaborate in a best case scenario, and downright frightening in a worst case scenario. Knowing that health care will very likely make up a large proportion of your expenditures when retired makes planning for it crucial.

We will discuss issues like Medicare, employer sponsored benefits, out of pocket expenses, and home health aides. We'll talk about determining factors like age, health, and you and your spouse's family health history. We will use existing data and statistics and forecast as efficiently as possible future issues, costs, and trends. To put it mildly, it's kind of a big deal, so we'll take it seriously and give it everything we've got.

There is good news though. I make it a big part of my job to have the answers to this question and all of the other questions about health care and retirement. I will go over some of the details further down the road in this book and assure you that there is a solution that makes sense to all of the problems related to paying for health care in retirement. And I promise you that my team and I stay up to date so that your plans can adapt to whatever changes or obstacles come about.

3. WHAT SHOULD I KNOW ABOUT MY RETIREMENT PLAN?

This can be a daunting and confusing question, but don't worry. Although there are many types of retirement plans out there, there are also many readily available options. This book will outline many of them. Naturally, the best way to determine which plan is best suited for your needs is to meet with you personally, but after reading this book I believe you will come away with a better than basic knowledge of what to expect, what questions to ask, and how to proceed. I'll go over Defined Benefit (DB) Plans, Defined Contribution (DC) Plans, Hybrid Retirement Plans, and Supplemental Retirement Plans. It might seem complicated, but I'll break it down into easier to digest pieces. I promise that you will come away feeling informed and confident.

4. SHOULD I CONSIDER AN EARLY RETIREMENT PACKAGE?

The decision to accept a "buy out" or Early Retirement Package is complex. But guess what? I've got you covered.

These lump-sum distributions are usually based on your age, service, and contract. Whether or not to accept them or turn them down is different for everyone. Sometimes it makes financial sense. In some cases, you should turn them down.

We'll look at all the factors that need to be considered when deciding this matter. Issues like how early retirement will affect your pension benefits and other retirement income. When the appropriate time to start taking Social Security benefits is, does the buy-out come with low or no cost health care insurance until you are eligible for Medicare, and where you are at with your savings and investments will be covered in this chapter. We will examine the tax implications as well as the health of your employer in order to mitigate the risk of a future layoff. When all is said and done, you will be able to navigate this tough question with ease.

5. WHAT DOES A DREAM RETIREMENT LOOK LIKE?

Is relaxation, rocking chairs, and fishing with the grandkids your idea of retirement? Are you more of a travel the world, ride across the country on your motorcycle, jump out of a perfectly good airplane, and start a new business kind of person? Maybe you like the idea of a bit of both. Whatever the case may be for you, you've worked hard, and your dreams should be achievable. I'll help set you on the course to accomplishing whatever your dream retirement looks like. Further into this book, I'll discuss places to live in retirement where the dollar stretches further. Whether you're stretched out on a tropical beach, relaxing in a European hamlet, or living the dream right here in the U.S.A., I've done the research so that you don't have to.

6. HOW CAN A FINANCIAL CONSULTANT HELP ME?

Planning for retirement is like an expedition. Sometimes it may even seem more akin to a battle. And you wouldn't plan an exploratory trip to the South Pole or take on a hostile force without a strategy. A good financial consultant can help you strategize for your dream retirement. I do this by maximizing your income potential while managing your risk. This is partly accomplished by putting together a suitable plan for your retirement goals, smoothing over the process of the transition into retirement, and helping to make sure that your dream retirement is fully accomplished.

Through years of experience helping over 700 households manage this process I've learned a lot. Most importantly, I've learned how to avoid the pitfalls that trap and misguide so many people in their retirement planning. But remember, it is my job as the navigator to help guide you, the captain of this ship, in reaching your desired destination. And if you let me, I'll do just that.

***

As we close out this first chapter on our voyage to understanding retirement planning for union workers, I want to remind you that it is all about endurance. Remember, life is a marathon, not a sprint. With good planning you'll have direction to make it to the finish line while enjoying the journey.

THE RETIREMENT RED ZONE

If you've ever spent any amount of time at a pub somewhere in America, I'm sure you've overheard this conversation: "Who's the greatest quarterback of all time?"

Essentially they're asking you to determine who is the best at football's most important position? Most folk's shortlist will mention Peyton Manning or Tom Brady. Or older players, from eras gone by consistently make the cut. Players like Otto Graham, Unitas, Bradshaw, Elway, and Marino. But one name you'll almost always hear on this greatest ever list is Joe Montana.

Why is that? Joe Montana's numbers aren't as great as other's that are frequently listed. Not all of his statistics add up to supreme greatness. He never led the league in passing. He never had 4,000 passing yards in a season. What made Montana so great was that he played his best when it mattered most. In four Super Bowls he had eleven touchdowns and zero interceptions. He won every Super Bowl he played in, and in three of them was awarded most valuable player. When the game was on the line, when the pressure was at its peak, Joe Montana performed. It's how he got his nickname, Joe Cool.

In terms of your finances, you want your money to perform at its peak level when the pressure is the greatest. When is that? It's when you are near your retirement target date. In the NFL they have an area of the field called the red zone. The red zone is when the offense drives the ball into their opponent's 20 yard line. It signifies that the offense is closing in on scoring points. And the red zone is precisely where you want your team to perform its best. The same goes for retirement planning. As you near your retirement date, as you reach your retirement red zone, you want your financial plans to score big for you.

The retirement red zone is mostly measured in the years before you plan on retiring, but there are some other factors that tell you that you are in the retirement red zone. To break it down as simply as possible, things get urgent within five to ten years of your retirement date. When you reach this point, you had better have a path defined. That is not to say that you can't still fix the mistakes of the past because in most instances you can. But it is to say that it is very important that your plan be entirely in place.

I'm not knocking anyone, especially hardworking seniors, but unless your ideal retirement is working as a greeter at Walmart just to make ends meet, then you'd better not screw up once you hit the retirement red zone.

Not to worry though, telling the masses hello and goodbye whilst trying to tag returns can be avoided. And one of the ways to avoid having to do something that you might not necessarily want to do, is to ensure that the date you set for retirement is well thought out and appropriate for your unique financial situation. Quitting your job may be high on your list of things to do, but let's do it for effect, not affect. That is to say, let's do it based on what it will accomplish, not just for the action of doing it. I hope you understand that this analogy is more than a grammar lesson. It is a crucial retirement planning lesson.

Another example of the retirement red zone's importance came in the crash of 2007/2008. Many people were heavily invested in traditional stocks and bonds, the value of which dropped to low levels during the recession. Those people who were not diversified properly had a very rude awakening. To say the least, they were caught off guard. To say it more plainly, they failed to have life's "what ifs" covered.

My solution to that involves being proactive, not reactive. It is about being aware that events like the one that took place in 2007/2008 and the systemic causes of it, can happen again, and suddenly. And the only way to ensure your money is in the safest possible harbor is to be fully engaged. There must be a plan to combat the proverbial "rainy day" or unforeseen circumstances that lead to an off market. This is, in part, accomplished by what I call having a "bucket" filled with low risk investments.

Think of it like this: when that rainy day hits, imagine you're in your boat, safely floating in your harbor. All of a sudden the boat starts filling with water. That "bucket" will bail you out. Low risk investments can help keep you afloat so that you can weather the storm.

So we've covered the idea of what the retirement red zone is and what you can do to protect yourself from losing the game. We know that the red zone is when most people get serious about thinking about retirement planning. But I don't think you can plan for retirement too early. The idea of mapping out each year, keeping your eye on the prize makes a lot of sense. After all, you don't want to panic before kick off in the Super Bowl. If you don't have a plan, you'll find yourself scrambling. If you want to play it cool, it's crucial for union workers like yourself to have an educated opinion about retirement options. Let's huddle up for a moment and draw a few plays. Let's develop a strategy and ensure we have a comfortable retirement plan in place.

But before we do that, let me call a timeout. What if I told you that you could retire at a much younger age if you were to put away just an extra hundred dollars a month? Would you do it? I always tell my younger clients the same thing. In the end, you will think one of two things: "I am glad I listened to Dan." Or, "I wish I had listened to Dan." Let's make sure that you end up saying the first one and not the second. Because, if your investments are symbolized by the quarterback in the retirement red zone, your financial consultant had better be a winning coach.

As a financial consultant focused on helping union workers, one of the most common questions I get is, "When can I afford to retire?" More than ever, retirees and pre-retirees in union trades have an added stress in retirement planning. Dealing with complex benefits packages and ever-changing options can really make planning for retirement stressful and a big whopping headache.

Don't worry though, I've got this covered, and soon you will too. There are some important things to keep in mind. For example, be thinking about the following ages: 55, 59 ½, 62, 66, and 70 ½.

At 55 many plans allow a union worker to have access to funds in some of their retirement plans. At 59 ½ most everyone has expanded options in their retirement plans along with an option to draw on funds without penalty. At 62 most are eligible for Social Security and each year that you don't take that out you get a potential pay raise for the future. At 66 you are at full Social Security retirement age and can receive benefits with no restrictions on income. And lastly, at 70 ½ if you have not started taking money out of your qualified retirement accounts you will have to, as the government demands that you take required minimum distributions (RMDs).

In addition to being confusing and stressful, when and how to retire can be emotionally draining. You've spent a lifetime committed to working and helping others achieve their goals. It can be tough to think about yourself.

We as Americans build up this idea of retirement, but many have not taken the time to truly think about what that means. In some cases it means sitting on the back porch smoking a cigar. In other cases it means traveling the globe. Either way, you need to prepare for the transition from working to ensure that it is the happiest time of your life. This also is helpful in mapping out the budget through retirement, particularly from ages 55 to 75 where the income stream has to be the most resilient. Going from working full time to being without work can cause undue anxiety. As well, the realization that your previous job will continue without your efforts can be hard to take. With that said, having a plan that allows you to fulfill your purpose in this next chapter of your life, will help alleviate some of those unneeded anxieties.

When you combine the financial questions and worries with the mixed emotions boiling inside you, it's no wonder so many people put off a retirement strategy until the very end.

It's okay to be fearful of retirement planning. Believe it or not, the average American is more fearful of losing their financial security than they are of death! That is why it is so utterly important that you find the right person to help with this daunting task. Someone who will unmask the boogey man and expose everything, right or wrong. Sure it may be a scary thought to see behind the curtain, and you may feel that your personal situation is far worse than that of others, but rest easy. The truth is there is no boogey man. Even the great and powerful Wizard of Oz was just a man with flashing lights and a loudspeaker.

Through it all, I can tell you this, I've had many people come into my office with what I call their financial junk drawer, turn it upside down and dump it all on my desk. Each time this happens, they end up sighing in relief afterwards and exclaiming that they wish that they had done it a long time ago. So whether you are considering retirement soon or even if it is a long way off, I can tell you that it is time to have that chat.

You may not like to think about the possibility of unpleasant things happening in your life, but should they happen, they will be a lot more palatable if you have a plan for them. Things like a disability or even a death. With the proper plan you can ensure that your family is taken care of. I know that for most people that is very important, just as it is for me. As well other unpleasant events like an unforeseen divorce and or having to move from your home can have a large impact if not planned for in advance.

Many of the measures that we use to help people decide when to retire are based on resources, and of course, desires. For instance, if you are like me, and love your job, then the timeline is not as important as compared to someone who dislikes their work.

This is where I'll tell you about Al. Some years ago, I got a call from an almost frantic gentleman named Al. He worked for a major company that you would surely recognize if named. Al was extremely frustrated at work. He had worked with stock brokers and financial people before, but felt as though he had not found the right one. A client of mine, and a friend of his, told him that I would be the right guy to talk to. So we scheduled some time to get together. This is when he gave me all of his information and dumped his proverbial financial junk drawer on my desk. This drawer had been compiled over 30 years. Then he asked if I would be able to give him a plan in which he would be able to retire…by the end of the month!

I went back to my team and crunched the numbers and ran Al and his family's situation through our process. A week later, I was sitting with Al and told him that he could retire at the end of the month. As you could guess, this was music to Al's ears. The thought of telling his employer that he would be retiring made him very happy to say the least. The funny thing about the rest of this story is that Al worked for six more years. It seems that once Al knew he had the power to walk away it changed from something that he had to do to something he could do. In his mind, something magical happened and work wasn't quite so bad anymore.

So don't stress. With a few simple questions you can know if you are on-track financially to meet your retirement goals. Here are a few considerations that can help you know if you have the potential to retire comfortably.

QUESTION	CONSIDERATION
Can I retire with debt?	The higher the debt, the greater your retirement expenses will be. Many Americans are retiring with high levels of debt
What are my projected retirement expenses?	This ranges from basic needs like housing and food, to lifestyle expenses like travel and entertainment
What sources of income do I have?	There are many. Social security, benefits and pension, rental properties and part time work, are just a few of many

Let's take a moment to look at these in greater detail.

CAN I RETIRE WITH DEBT?

In many instances people retire with debts like mortgages, car payments, and maybe even student loans that they are paying on behalf of their children or grandchildren. Some debts even have tax advantages associated with them. With the right planning in place, retiring while carrying debt, although not ideal, can be managed and serviced without disrupting lifestyle.

WHAT ARE MY RETIREMENT EXPENSES?

Although there are some basic expenses that prove to be true across the board for all retirees, determining your expenses in retirement depends upon the individual and their choice of and level of lifestyle. Some factors that determine your expenses are where you live, health care costs, what activities you partake in, and generally how "high on the hog" you choose to live. Other issues to consider when planning how to handle your expenses in retirement include provisions for unforeseen medical needs and long-term care issues.

WHAT SOURCES OF INCOME DO I HAVE?

Some retirees retire to a new career or another job. Some start businesses and have income from those ventures. Whether a new career or starting a business are in your future, many of you will have in addition to Social Security, pensions and income from investments. Make sure to check out the chapters on Social Security and retirement investment plans later in this book.

The truth of the matter is that planning for retirement doesn't come with an easy to follow playbook. There is no simple formula that works for everyone. Unfortunately, when you find yourself in the red zone there isn't much room for error. That doesn't mean that the sky is falling either. It just means that the main reason people always throw the keys to me in the hopes of getting home in one piece, is because they know I have the knowledge and skills to help get them home.

When it comes to putting together a plan that makes sense for your individual needs, whatever they may be, I can promise you that I've done the research, helped a lot of people achieve the retirement of their dreams, and next to you, am the person who cares most about your money.

CAN I AFFORD TO RETIRE CHECKLIST

What are my planned budget and lifestyle expectations?

What's my Social Security income?

What are my pension plans?

Do I have any potential inheritances?

Have I considered my non-qualified assets?

Do I have retirement plan assets?

What are my other income sources?

How much current debt do I have?

WHAT DOES MY DREAM RETIREMENT LOOK LIKE?

In a multi-decade study Harvard sociologist, Dr. Edward Banfield, sought to better understand why some people become wildly successful, while most did not. His research uncovered some surprising findings. Factors like intelligence, family background, and access to influential contacts had little to do with determining someone's success. What he discovered was that most successful people had a similar attitude. Most had the same frame of mind.

Dr. Banfield labeled this mindset the attitude of "long-time perspective." He concluded that the people who were the most successful in life were those who took a long-term outlook. People who took the future into consideration with each present day decision were more likely to move up in life. By thinking of the future, they were more likely to endure present hardships and do the difficult tasks required to move ahead.

Thinking on that now, it makes perfect sense. When you have your eye on a prize, when there's a goal that you're fixed on, you're less likely to quit. A small bump in the road or patch of hard times are easier to endure when you are fixated on your destination.

With Dr. Banfield's longtime perspective in mind, let's think about your retirement. What does your dream retirement look like? Take a moment to relax. Picture yourself at ease. What kind of weather surrounds you? What are the sights, sounds, and smells that greet you as you watch the day pass? Are you alone? Are you spending more time with loved ones? Or maybe you're out exploring and enjoying your passions.

There is no right or wrong here. It's about you and what makes you happiest. Everyone's retirement dream is different. But it's more than just a dream. Thinking about what your perfect retirement looks like is an important exercise. Knowing what you want is a key aspect of strategizing your retirement planning. Why not take a moment to dream about it? It's only the rest of your life.

Perhaps you have pursuits that you have not yet had time to act upon. The dream of learning to play a musical instrument, maybe even to be in a band. Or perhaps you desire to learn a new language or other type of skill. Some of you may even want to go back to school. Did you know that many universities offer free classes to seniors?

Maybe your dream retirement involves adventure and travel. To go off and explore. See the world. Relax on a beautiful beach in French Polynesia. Go on a wildlife safari in Africa. View the Northern Lights. Or for those with a real wanderlust, maybe sailing around the world is your idea of a dream retirement.

For some of you, none of the aforementioned things will be on your personal bucket list. Instead, maybe your dream retirement is relaxing with family and friends. Spending more time with your spouse, children, or grandchildren. Maybe for you, taking it as easy as possible is the appropriate reward for a lifetime of hard work.

Whatever the case, it doesn't really matter as long as you have the plan in place to do whatever it is that you want to do. And guess what, with the right planning, you can even decide to have multiple dream retirement scenarios. Perhaps a combination of globetrotting adventure and easy going relaxation with the family.

My job is to help you be secure in your retirement. But your job is to figure out what your dream retirement looks like.

Let me give you three different scenarios from a recent business trip of mine to Florida's Gulf Coast. For a long time I had been promising to visit a client in Tampa. Finally, my schedule allowed me that opportunity. So I flew down and figured that while I was there I would take the time to make some other visits.

I'm sure glad that I did. It was very gratifying to see individuals that I helped, living their versions of dream retirements. It was also eye opening. I'm happy that I can share these three different experiences with you now. Although they were all from the same trip to Florida, you will see that they showcase three very different situations.

SCENARIO ONE

My first stop was to visit a client of mine who had just recently retired. He had pondered the question of where to spend his winters for quite a while. When it came time for him to decide, one factor above all else played the most important role.

He wanted to be near his mother. This had been a living situation that he couldn't entertain while he was still among the ranks of the working. But it was very important to him in retirement. In fact, he considered it a luxury. He knew that he had missed a lot of family time over his career and he was well aware of the fact that time is fleeting, so he made this his highest priority.

He had spent a career as a high level executive who was very seldom in the same place for very long. Both his wife and he had put in long hours at their careers and had done so for quite some time.

Ironically, his wife had spent her career working for of all things, a financial consultant. Yet he came to me as a new client, right around the time he was to retire. The fact that he chose me to help him achieve his goals was flattering and I respected that he had done so. I crunched the numbers and in the end was able to help maximize the dollars that went into his pocket. As well, I did some strategic estate and tax planning for him and developed a plan for his health care options.

The work that my team and I did for him, allowed him to bring to reality his dream of spending his winters in Florida and in turn gave him the time with his mother that he had been wanting for so long. For him, this was a dream retirement.

SCENARIO TWO

The couple from my second example have been clients of mine for around five years. In that time, they always seemed to be eyeballing a retirement date that was, "Just around the corner." But they never seemed like they could pull the proverbial pin on it. The husband, Jack, was someone who identified himself with his job. Meanwhile, his wife had started spending a lot of time in Florida without him.

It came to my attention that Jack was always leaving vacation time unused. So when his wife, Janet, found a condo that struck both of their fancies, I knew I needed to give Jack a nudge. You see, Jack was unsure whether he could really pull the trigger on retirement. So I suggested that instead of taking one week of vacation down there, he take two. He did so and guess what, he liked it.

Then I suggested that he try three weeks of vacation. He did. And this time he even took the dog. He liked it even more.

This led to him reaching a comfortable place when it came to pulling the retirement lever. When I saw them at their Florida condo I became excited to learn that they were both very happy and that Jack was doing great in retirement.

SCENARIO THREE

My last example is about Craig and Susie. They've been talking about the place they winter for years. It happened to be an RV Resort, something I didn't know much about.

Well let me tell you in case you don't know much about RV Resorts either, I was so glad that this year I kept my promise to visit. Wow, their ideal winter place didn't disappoint. In fact it exceeded my expectations. More than an RV resort, it was a lifestyle community, with all of the fixings. It had something for everyone, from belly dancing classes to chess club. Karaoke, a pool, a movie theatre, synchronized swimming, restaurants and bars, a clubhouse, and so much more.

To put it lightly, they were not resting or sitting around during their retirement. In fact, it was quite the opposite. Their retirement is completely filled with activities. From cocktail parties and barbecues, to golf and learning experiences. I doubt that they would know what a dull moment even was.

***

There are numerous examples beyond the ones laid out here that illustrate how today's retirees can plan on living long, full, and active lives after they retire. No longer is retirement a slow ride off into the sunset. Instead, you're starting an exciting new chapter of your life. With a little dreaming, and the right planning and investments, you too can redefine what retirement means.

It seems as though here, in America, we build up the idea of retirement but often never get past the thinking stage. The question is what would, or will you do in retirement? Whether it's today or five years from now, what do you want out of life? You need to put some real thought into what you would actually like your retirement to be like.

Let's go back to Dr. Banfield's longtime perspective for a minute. In doing so, I think you will be able to see that just knowing that a retirement can truly be the fulfillment of a lifelong dream will make doing whatever it takes to get there a whole lot easier. Sure there are components like planning, saving, and investing involved in making a dream retirement a reality, but if you were to ask anyone who is living theirs, I know that they would tell you that it's all worth it.

In the next two chapters, we will have a discussion about places to retire should you be interested in living somewhere else. First, we will keep it close to home and talk about some great places to retire right here in the United States. Then we will cast our net farther afield and look at some terrific places for retirement abroad.

In both chapters we will touch on some of the advantages that certain locations offer. In discovering these factors, you just might find that your dream retirement involves packing up and moving. It isn't necessarily for everyone, but for some it can change the whole dynamic of retirement.

WHAT DOES MY DREAM RETIREMENT LOOK LIKE?

Does my dream retirement involve:

Travel?

Adventure?

Learning?

Working at a new career?

Relaxing?

Spending time with loved ones?

Or something unique to me?

WHERE SHOULD I RETIRE?

Real estate 101. Location, location, location. Even if you don't know a thing about buying a home, you probably know that being in the right location is paramount. What's the school district like? Is it in a good neighborhood? How's the freeway access? Is there a park nearby? Location matters.

But this popular axiom also rings true when it comes to retirement. Not only when, but where to retire is an important consideration. The state, county, and city you live in can contribute to the success and happiness you find in your much deserved retirement. Unlike, buying a conventional home, your retirement location requires a few special considerations.

Let's look at a few details to better determine the best place for you.

KEY QUESTION	CONSIDERATION
What is the cost of living where I'll live?	- Cost of living is expressed as an index - Keep in mind that 100 is the national average

KEY QUESTION	CONSIDERATION
What are the state's taxes like?	- A low tax rate for a worker isn't always a low tax rate for a retiree - Sales and real estate levies hit retirees harder - Consider states with special breaks for seniors and retirees
How robust is the economy?	- Strong local economies typically raise home values - Look for areas with lower unemployment rates
Do I have comfortable access to good health care?	- As you age, accessibility to health care may become more important to you - Areas with clean air, clean water, and weather that encourages activity may help you maintain your good health
How safe is the neighborhood?	- A good marker for accessing is looking at the violent crime rate - The Federal Bureau of Investigation provides detailed reports and figures on violent crime rates
Does my neighborhood provide a community that promotes health?	- Walkable and bike friendly communities encourage more activity activity and can promote better health as you age

Right about now you may be thinking that is a lot to digest. Let's take a closer look at these one at a time

WHAT IS THE COST OF LIVING WHERE I'LL LIVE?

Cost of living indexes factor in average expenses for transportation, food, energy, shelter, health care, child care, education, and entertainment for a particular area. For instance, it is much less costly to live in Omaha, Nebraska than it is to live in San Francisco, California. When it comes to making your money stretch it is advisable to figure in the cost of living for the area or city where you intend to live.

Let's face it, everything seems to be getting more and more expensive these days. And if you are someone that wants to have an active retirement, doing some research into where you get the most bang for your buck while not sacrificing other favorable factors like climate, safety, and entertainment options is always a good idea. With a little effort, settling on a location that offers what you are looking for but remains within your budget is easily achievable. For instance, if you have lived your working years in a place that sees hard and cold winters and want to spend your retirement years in a better climate, I assure you that you can. But you might have to pick a smaller city over a large metropolitan area.

For instance, there are numerous smaller and less expensive cities in Florida than Miami or Ft. Myers that still have a warm climate, proximity to the beach, and many entertainment options. The same goes for other sunny locales like Arizona, California, and Texas.

Although there isn't an official cost of living index prepared by the U.S. government, many unofficial parties produce reports that monitor the costs of living across the United States[1]. Comparing the national average to the area you are considering is a good idea. If the average is 100, be careful of areas that creep above a cost of living index over 105.

CITIES WITH A GREAT COST OF LIVING INDEX:
- Memphis, Tennessee
- San Antonio, Texas
- Salt Lake City, Utah

WHAT ARE THE STATE TAXES LIKE?

Something to consider: while states like Texas, Florida, and Alaska may have appealing broad tax plans, higher taxes, sales taxes, and increased rates for real estate may hit retirees harder. Consider states that offer breaks and incentives to retirees and seniors. Sure, most of us have heard that Texas and Florida are great states for retirees. But there are other states you may not have considered that offer great benefits. There are seven states that don't have any income tax and two more that only tax income from interest and dividends.

STATES WITH NO INCOME TAX:
- Wyoming
- Florida
- Nevada
- Alaska

---

[1] *These lists of favorable places were formed compiling 2015-2017 data and statistics from Forbes, Kiplinger, Sperling's Best Places, NAHB Housing Opportunity Index, AARP, Business Insider, and the FBI database. Places change with the times and shifting political landscape. Please consult a financial consultant for the most up to date considerations discussed in this chapter.*

- Washington
- South Dakota
- Texas

STATES THAT ONLY TAX INCOME FROM INTEREST AND DIVIDENDS:
- New Hampshire
- Tennessee

For many of you, retiring only means leaving your current employment. As you just might be looking forward to working at something else. As well, income earned from investment interest and dividends is a reality. Choosing a location in a state with favorable income tax may still be a pertinent issue.

Property tax might also be an issue to explore. If you plan on owning your home, taking an in depth look at the most favorable states for property tax rates is a necessity.

STATES WITH THE LOWEST PROPERTY TAXES IN ORDER STARTING WITH THE LOWEST RATES:
- Louisiana
- Alabama
- West Virginia
- Arkansas
- South Carolina
- Mississippi
- New Mexico
- Delaware
- Oklahoma
- Arizona

STATES WITH THE HIGHEST PROPERTY TAXES IN ORDER FROM THE HIGHEST RATES:
- New Jersey
- New Hampshire
- Connecticut
- Vermont
- New York
- Rhode Island
- Illinois
- Massachusetts
- Wisconsin
- Nebraska

Taking a good look at sales tax rates can also be important. For instance, the states of Delaware, New Hampshire, and Oregon all have a 0% sales tax rate, whereas, Illinois, California, and Arizona have sales tax rates over 10%. Exploring how a given states sales tax rates could have an effect on your budget is something that a good financial consultant can help you do. And the same goes for the other types of taxes and what kinds of effects they can have on your retirement.

HOW ROBUST IS THE ECONOMY?

If you have ever studied the natural world then you know that the health of an ecosystem is very important. You will also know that there are many factors that play a role in determining whether the ecosystem is healthy. Think of where you live or might want to live as an ecosystem as well. Economic factors can have a huge effect on the overall health of a given location. If unemployment is high, then crime rates are generally high, which in turn has an effect on the prospects for your safety. You most likely want to look for an area that has a better unemployment rate than the national average. Strong economies typically hold better housing prices, and promote safer living. They also offer more in the way of entertainment options, are more conducive to healthy living, and promote a better overall quality of life.

AREAS WITH PROLONGED AND SUSTAINED STRONG ECONOMIES:
- Fort Collins, Colorado
- Salt Lake City, Utah
- Charleston, South Carolina
- Cedar Rapids, Iowa

DO I HAVE COMFORTABLE ACCESS TO GOOD HEALTH CARE?

As you age, access and availability to good health care becomes more and more important. Some places are much better than others when it comes to health care. And even more to the point, some places are downright scary when it comes to their lack of physicians and health care facilities. One good way to measure a location's health care facilities is by the number of physicians per capita.

CITIES WITH A HIGH PHYSICIANS PER CAPITA RATE:
- Saline, Michigan
- Blowing Rock, North Carolina
- Cherokee, North Carolina
- Dillingham, Alaska
- Wrangell, Alaska
- Livermore, California

- Anson, Texas
- Petersburg, Alaska
- San Leandro, California
- Tyrone, Pennsylvania

HOW SAFE IS THE NEIGHBORHOOD?

Let's face it, nobody wants to live in a place where they don't feel safe. Additionally, safer neighborhoods, and in general cities with lower violent crime rates, maintain higher property values and better qualities of life. So if relocating is on your radar, do a little research into crime rates for all of your prospective destinations. Here are a few examples of cities with low violent crime rates. You can do a more thorough search on the FBI's website, FBI.gov.

CITIES WITH THE LOW VIOLENT CRIME RATES:
- Cape Coral, Florida
- Honolulu, Hawaii
- Bellevue, Washington

DOES MY NEIGHBORHOOD AND COMMUNITY PROMOTE GOOD HEALTH?

Consider things like walking and biking, or fair weather that invites you to maintain an active lifestyle. Websites like redfin.com allows you to quickly search how your city fares at being walkable and transit friendly. Are there farmers markets, shops, and errands you can run by foot? These activities can help promote a longer and healthier life. Obviously bigger cities will have the best walkability scores. New York, San Francisco, and Boston typically top the charts year after year. But there are some other cities that may surprise you in their pedestrian friendliness.

MORE CITIES WITH HIGH WALKING SCORES:
- St. Louis, Missouri
- Rochester, New York
- Providence, Rhode Island

A quick internet search can instantly field you a list of places to retire. But hopefully the questions we asked here can help you better navigate which city best fits your needs. So whether you imagine yourself in the outdoor activity capital of Boulder, Colorado, or in a sleepy beach town in the Carolinas, or somewhere completely different from both of those, the point is America offers a vast array of options. Just make sure to do your homework and prioritize what qualities in a place to live are most important to you.

WHERE SHOULD I RETIRE?

Consider these qualities when selecting your retirement locale:

What is the cost of living like?

What are the state income taxes like?

What are the sales and property taxes like?

Does it have good access to health care?

Is it safe?

Is it walkable?

What is the climate like?

CAN I RETIRE ABROAD?

As of 2016, the Social Security Administration states that just under 400,000 American retirees are now living abroad. Most often, the countries they are moving to are Japan, Canada, Mexico, the United Kingdom, and Germany.

The rationale most retirees give for moving beyond the U.S. borders are cost of living. In many cases, beach cities outside the United States can stretch your dollar. But there's a great big world out there. Let's look at a few questions to ask if you should think about retiring abroad. And for a little fun, let's think about some places you may not have considered for that exotic place to retire[2].

---

[2]*Like the last chapter, these lists of cities and countries are based on a conglomerate of statistics and data sourced from articles and online resources including: the Department of State, Social Security Administration, Kiplinger, Investopia, Forbes, Merrill Lynch, USA Today, Bankrate, AARP, Business Insider, and International Living. While these listed suggestions are a great starting point in getting you to think about retiring abroad, please consult a financial or tax consultant for the most up-to-date information.*

HURDLES	STRATEGIES
Will there be a language barrier?	- Most of the world speaks some English - There is more affordable access to robust language curriculum than ever before
Can I integrate with the local culture?	- As an expatriate you can expect to feel some isolation in a new community - Spend a few months in the area before you move - Consider areas with more expatriates - Energetic communities can aid in feeling more a part of the culture
Is quality health care accessible?	- As you age, health care quality and costs become more important - While there is accessibility to great health care abroad, quality can vary greatly city to city
What is the cost of living difference?	- Talk to your financial consultant to discuss how living abroad can affect your portfolio - Don't forget to add up relocation costs, furnishings, utilities, and amenities when comparing your domestic and foreign budgets
Are there any tax advantages abroad?	- Remember, the IRS taxes U.S. citizens on their income no matter where they live - Some countries offer tax treaties

WILL THERE BE A LANGUAGE BARRIER?

English is widely spoken around the world, but still, language can be a barrier to living the best quality of life when abroad. Many places have large expat communities, where the English language is very common, sometimes even more prevalently spoken than the native language. In many communities like southern Spain, coastal Portugal, and throughout Costa Rica and Panama, English speaking expat communities thrive.

For those of you looking to get more immersed, wanting to live like a local, there are numerous ways to learn a second language. With an abundance of language learning courses, tutors, community college offerings, and even free language learning apps on your phone, don't be scared off by the thought of having to learn a foreign language. Actually, I'm sure many of you would find it to be an exciting challenge, where the rewards are exotic locales, tropical beaches, and cosmopolitan culture capitals.

COUNTIES WITH HIGH ENGLISH SPEAKING POPULATIONS:
- Canada
- Australia
- New Zealand
- United Kingdom
- Italy
- Spain
- Brazil

CAN I INTEGRATE WITH THE LOCAL CULTURE?

The answer to this question depends on your mentality and the culture of the place you are considering. Western minded countries like those in the Caribbean, Western Europe, as well as Australia, New Zealand, and Canada are all pretty close in values and laws to what you are used to in the United States. Latin American countries can be great on the cost of living index, but there definitely exists a difference in culture and established legal systems.

Less popular locations can be found in Asia, Africa, and the Middle East. Some of these places, such as Thailand, have very interesting offerings for retirees like VIP residency programs. These programs come with many perks including a concierge to handle all kinds of needs like cutting through the red tape. Choosing a more exotic location depends on your interest level. But for a few of you, relocating to somewhere exotic that stretches your dollar might be something you are keen to do.

Obviously Canada, Mexico, and Europe are popular destinations. Here are a few more that Americans are moving to in retirement.

COUNTRIES WITH HIGHER U.S. EXPATRIATE POPULATIONS
- Israel
- Brazil
- The Philippines
- Dominican Republic
- Japan
- Colombia
- China and Hong Kong

DO I HAVE COMFORTABLE ACCESS TO GOOD HEALTH CARE?

Once again a great measurement to go by is physicians per capita. Many countries can have variance in the quality of health care city to city. If you require specialty care, you may need to budget for travel and extended lodging.

FOREIGN COUNTRIES WITH ROBUST HEALTH CARE SYSTEMS:
- Sweden
- Denmark
- Netherlands
- United Kingdom
- Canada
- New Zealand
- Austria
- Australia
- Uruguay

WHAT'S THE COST OF LIVING DIFFERENCE?

Some of the factors that have to be considered in budgeting a true cost of living difference between living abroad and living in the United States are things like cellphone plans, cable, utilities, and groceries. These factors can be wildly expensive compared to domestic rates. Consider the cost of moving. As you know, moving is much more than just getting a place. How will you furnish it? Will you be driving? These things can add up in a hurry.

BEACHFRONT COUNTRIES WITH LOWER COST OF LIVING:
- Thailand
- Portugal

- Panama
- Belize
- Malaysia

WHAT ARE THE TAX ADVANTAGES TO LIVING ABROAD?

The IRS taxes U.S. Citizens no matter where they live. In most instances you are expected to file an income tax return, even if you live in a tax-free country like the Cayman Islands. Some countries offer tax treaties with the United States that help you avoid being double taxed. Many more places offer treaties than just Canada and Mexico.

COUNTRIES WITH U.S. TAX TREATIES:
- South Africa
- Japan
- Venezuela
- Barbados
- Italy
- Iceland
- Israel

I urge you to consult with a financial consultant or tax advisor to discuss portfolio and tax implications in regards to the countries you may be considering.

As I've said before, it's never too early to dream. And it never hurts to explore what your options are, even if you never end up using them. To get you started with your dreaming, here are five cities that might satisfy your thirst for adventure and romance.

FIVE CITIES FOR RETIRING ABROAD:

1. ALGARVE, PORTUGAL

With a great climate, large expat community, and beautiful beaches, this city ranks high on just about everyone's list for retiring abroad.

2. LAS TERRENAS, DOMINICAN REPUBLIC

What do you think about white sand beaches and French restaurants? I think it sounds amazing.

3. PAU, FRANCE

Located in the southwestern Basque area of France, near the Spanish border, this area is the type of lush French countryside that retirement dreams are made of. Perhaps that is why so many Brits have been calling it home for such a long time.

4. CHIANG MAI, THAILAND

How would you like to live like the King and Queen of Siam on just $1,100 a month? Well, in the history rich, exotic, and bustling international city of Chiang Mai you can do just that.

5. PLAYA DEL CARMEN, MEXICO

If turquoise Caribbean waters, beautiful beaches, and great scuba diving sounds appealing then Playa del Carmen might just be the spot for you. It already hosts a large expat community, making integration into the area even easier for newcomers.

IS RETIRING OUTSIDE THE U.S. RIGHT FOR ME?

Cost of living abroad can be considerably less than in the U.S.

A Strong U.S. dollar can get you a lot more bang for your buck

Vibrant cities, beautiful beach towns, and culture abound in many locations

Language can be a barrier, but can be overcome

Explore tax implications with your financial consultant

Health care is always an issue to thoroughly research, but often-times you can receive first world care at a vast discount

WHAT SHOULD I KNOW ABOUT MY RETIREMENT PLAN?

Let's imagine for a moment that you're on a ski vacation. Picture yourself at the very peak of the mountain. The view from up top is spectacular. And racing down the mountain seems like a great idea, but you may want to talk to someone who has done the run to get a better idea of what lies ahead.

From this vantage point, you can choose any path down the mountain you want. But if you've never been to this resort, or say you don't have a trail map with you, it might behoove you to ask a local or a guide for some advice getting down.

But what good would their advice be if they didn't know anything about you? Say you're a complete novice, but the guide sends you down a steep double black run with cliffs and rocks, because it was his favorite route. That wouldn't be much fun. Or what if they didn't know that you had a bum knee, so they send you down a slope pocked with knee bruising moguls. Or maybe you were hoping to capture that perfect picture, but he doesn't send you toward the scenic route.

Without knowing the particulars, the details and goals, it's difficult to have a plan or a route in place that best meets your needs. The same goes for your retirement plan. To have the best time, to get the satisfaction you want, the joy that indulges your specific and wholly individual needs, you need to know the details of your retirement plan. With that in mind, let's take a moment to consider your retirement plan before we go charging down that mountain.

These days there seems to be a myriad of retirement plans and options out there. And the list keeps growing. It's no surprise how confusing and overwhelming this can be for the worker. Obviously, the best way to address your concerns and questions is to meet personally with a financial consultant, but in lieu of a chat, I've come up with a quick list of common retirement plan types. And to help you navigate past the bumps and steeps you may encounter, I've provided a few special concerns you may want to think about. Let's get to it.

MAJOR PLANS	KEY COMPONENTS
Defined Benefit (DB) Plans	- May guarantee a lifetime retirement benefit - Must consider factors like age, years of employment, and salary - DB Plans are becoming less common
Defined Contribution (DC) Plans	- DC plans are the most popular type of employer-sponsored retirement plans - For union workers the most common type of DC Plan is 401(k) - You decide how much to contribute

| Hybrid Retirement Plans | - Combines features of the DB and DC Plans
- Employees may receive a stream of income or lump-sum distribution at retirement |
| Supplemental Retirement Plans | - Allow you to save beyond what's contributed by your primary plan
- Contribution limits, early with-drawal penalties, and many details will vary
- Best to review this plan with a financial consultant |

You know the drill. Let's take a look at these four plans in greater detail.

WHAT IS A DEFINED BENEFIT PLAN?

With a defined benefit plan the employer is responsible to deliver a set amount per month to the employee or employee's spouse, typically until the entitled person is deceased. Once a promise in this situation is made, the responsible party, whether a union or an employer is required to provide said income to the participant, and if they fail to maintain the ability to follow through on this promise, they would find themselves met with stern repercussions. In the case of the entitled person dying, benefits can be passed on to their spouse if certain criteria are in place ahead of time. As an example, a person who chooses a spousal continuation benefit could leave unto their spouse benefits for many years.

GREAT. SO THEN WHAT'S A DEFINED CONTRIBUTION PLAN?

The Defined Contribution Plan makes no promise of what you will receive. Instead, the benefactor promises what they will contribute (a certain amount) in present time to the plan and provides that the entitled individual will have access in some measure depending upon the performance of the plan's investments, leading to a far less predictable outcome than the defined benefit plan. However, the entitled individual often has an ability to guide how what is contributed on their behalf be invested.

WHAT SHOULD I CONSIDER WITH HYBRID RETIREMENT PLANS?

Hybrid Retirement Plans often allow the participant to choose the path they prefer. This allows more flexibility for the participant. Some individuals will choose an income stream without the burden of responsibility, while others choose to have more control of their investments. These types of plans offer more flexibility than either of the aforementioned types of plans.

ARE THERE DIFFERENT FACTORS TO TAKE INTO ACCOUNT WITH SUPPLEMENTAL RETIREMENT PLANS?

With Supplemental Retirement Plans the intention is to be able to give the employee the ability to save beyond normal programs. Based upon the objective of the participant these types of plans allow additional funding but often are more restrictive with access to funds and lack flexibility.

WAIT A MINUTE. WHAT ABOUT SOCIAL SECURITY?

If you're confused about Social Security, trust me, you're not alone! In just the discussion of ages alone, 62, 66, and 70 are significant milestones, each with their own pros and cons. At age 62 most people become eligible to receive Social Security benefits, but are restricted in the amount of income they can earn while receiving these benefits, should they exceed the amount allowed. There are also negative consequences that result in higher taxes and a required payback.

At 66 you are no longer restricted by how much money you can earn while drawing Social Security benefits. Every year from age 62 to 70 that you put off collecting Social Security benefits you receive an 8% increase in your benefits. At age 70 you no longer benefit from waiting and therefore would begin to accept benefits.

It is always a good idea to refer to your financial consultant when deciding when to take the benefits as there is a calculator that we use that can project a suitable time based on multiple factors. In this regard, your individual situation is unique. Issues such as personal circumstances in matters of health and family longevity history can influence your decision when to begin to accept benefits. As an example, if you come from a long line of octogenarians, then waiting until you were 66 to tap into the Social Security well would make sense. As a financial consultant, I have vast experience in helping people with this complicated decision.

SHOULD I WORK AFTER RETIRING?

More and more I'm seeing clients retiring from work that they have to do and starting to work at something that they want to do. In these cases, we have very specific conversations based upon the income potential at the new career. If the new income is very insignificant, its impact on Social Security is nominal. However, as we have many union workers who retire and choose a pension option and then do what is referenced as double dipping, earning a sizable income while drawing on their pension, the Social Security deferment option becomes the obvious route.

We also have many clients who pursue a consulting path which may have an inconsistent income and must be planned for accordingly. With the increase in people living longer lives, we're also seeing an increase in people who are enjoying their new lives at work. Many of my client are looking at their retirement jobs as a new chapter. They're excited about them in the same way that they were with their apprenticeship programs so many years before.

SHOULD I ELECT TO USE A SURVIVOR BENEFIT OPTION FOR MY SPOUSE?

Although in this area there are some personal preferences factored into the decision making process, there are specific income maximization tools that we utilize. The natural instinct is to take the highest amount of income over one's life. But we've learned from experience that it is far more complicated than it appears on the surface. Doing just that might result in unintended negative consequences for your spouse, should you die before them. Therefore, since I have yet to meet an individual with a reliable crystal ball, I always like to thoroughly discuss the options for possible situations, regardless of how uncomfortable the subject matter may be.

There are options that can safeguard against leaving a loved one in the proverbial lurch. The intention here is to strike the balance between maximizing the lifetime income from our pension plan without jeopardizing the future of our family. It should be noted that almost all pension plans stop at one generation, meaning that if you are married, a spouse could potentially receive benefits from the pension if the proper measures are put in place. But keep in mind, very rarely do the benefits ever pass on to children or grandchildren.

DO I HAVE LIFE INSURANCE?
DO I NEED LIFE INSURANCE?

This is one of the more popular questions that I'm asked and I quickly steal a line from my partner Tim Croak. "People only buy life insurance for one of two reasons: they either owe somebody or love somebody." Although I want to agree with Tim, I have to tell you that sometimes the math just works. So every opportunity I have where someone else carries the risk rather than one of my clients, I seize that moment. With the continuation of longer lifetimes for individuals, it has done something that has never been done before in the insurance world. It has lowered the cost of premiums. Part of this is based on the insurance companies being able to hold the premiums longer and part of it is because of the increase in efficiency of these insurance products.

I often draw a parallel between a '65 Ford Mustang and a brand new Mustang. Both are a cool way to get around town, but the newer Mustang gets better than 30 miles per gallon. With the newest insurance, you pay less in premiums and get more in benefits.

In these new hybrid policies, they not only provide significantly less expensive ways to cover risk, they also have benefits that were previously not in existence. Benefits like long-term care or chronic illness riders are now available. This allows the individual to use these funds to pay for expenses rather than using retirement investments that often have hefty tax burdens attached.

BUT WAIT...THERE'S MORE!

Some of you may be participating in a Defined Benefit pension plan. This allows you to participate and select from different retirement income options and schedules. As your retirement date nears there are some crucial questions you'll want to think hard about. I've listed a few:

> How much income will I need in retirement?
>
> If there's a Deferred Retirement Option Program (DROP) available to me, is it worthwhile to continue working while my retirement benefits keep accumulating?
>
> What other sources of income do I have?
>
> How great is the age difference between me and my partner?
>
> Do I have health care insurance options? If so, what are they?

GOT TIME FOR A STORY? GOOD.

A client named James came into my office approximately five years prior to what he believed was his retirement date. We went through the money map process to chart the path for James and his wife, Janet. Through the process of wanting to maximize all of the optional benefits, we applied for life insurance on James. Now, when it came time to choose his pension options, we could answer all of his questions, laying out all of the options, allowing him to make the most informed decision.

In the process of the insurance underwriting, it was discovered that cancer was present in James' body. Although this quickly made everything else pale in the level of importance, my team quickly went to work to make amendments to James' retirement plan so James could focus on his recovery and his family, while retiring early. The point is that life can throw you an unexpected curve ball at any time. But with the right planning, you stand a better chance at not striking out.

DOING THE MATH. NOTHING IS MORE IMPORTANT.

The reason this chapter is so important, is because when the time comes, you only get to pull the proverbial lever once in the process. Even though you may have worked for thirty years, it all comes down to one decision in the end. And you don't get a do over if you mess it up. That is why it is so important that you come see me or someone like me before making the decision. You need to walk into it with all of the information possible so that you can, as the old knight in Indiana Jones and the Last Crusade would say, "Choose wisely."

You will quickly realize that I'm not the only one putting such emphasis on this decision. If you are married, you will no doubt have a bunch of signatures from people like your spouse and a notary signing off on this decision. So if you have come to this part of the book and have still not walked through these options with a financial consultant, you need to put this book down and call me now.

Here is an example to help illustrate something that most people don't understand. Rick has the number one option of receiving $4,000 dollars a month from his pension. If he were to opt to take the whole $4,000 a month, then his wife Nancy would receive nothing if he died. The benefits would cease.

However, if he decided to take only $3,500 a month, and if something happened to him, Nancy would then get $1,750. Likewise, if he decided on taking only $3,000 then his wife would get $3,000 a month if he were to die.

Alternatively, some decide to take a lump sum. In the case of Rick, the lump sum would total $912,000. This can look sexy at face value, but you need to do the math. If you don't have the desire to pass money on to your heirs, then this option would be less than ideal. Again it all comes down to the numbers and lucky for you we can help you with the equation. Being informed when making this decision is so important, because once this decision is made it can't be changed. You have to live with it, as does your spouse and your family.

***

With these questions and considerations you'll have a better idea how to navigate down the mountain. And more importantly, if you talk to a guide, you'll be equipped to provide them with the vital information they need to better help you enjoy your journey.

WHAT SHOULD I KNOW ABOUT MY RETIREMENT PLAN?

There is no going back once you pull the proverbial lever

You must do the math to ensure that your loved ones are taken care of

It's all in the numbers, they don't lie

A financial consultant can help you "choose wisely"

Don't make decisions based on how "sexy" they look

401(K) AND ROTH IRA. WHAT'S THE DIFFERENCE?

WHAT'S A 401(k)?

Take a guess. Which section of the IRS tax code defines a 401(k)? If you guessed section 401(k) you are correct. That's where the strange name comes from.

At the basic level a 401(k) is an employer-sponsored deferred contribution retirement plan. The way it works is simple enough. You elect to sign up for a 401(k) plan through your employer. Then you select the investment options that work best for you within the plan. Next, your workplace takes a portion of funds out of your paycheck before income taxes are withdrawn and deposits the amount in your plan. In some instances, as an added incentive, your 401(k) contributions are matched by your employer.

So how do you get your money? Simple. When you reach retirement age, you take your money out of the 401(k). However, when you withdraw from your 401(k) that money is subject to income tax. Since you didn't pay taxes on those funds earlier, the IRS taxes you later when you withdraw. If you're paying taxes either way on the money, what's the big deal with 401(k)? When you defer your taxes until later down the road, the assumption is that you will be in a much lower tax bracket at retirement age than when you are in your prime earning years.

As it stands, there's no limit on the income level of a person who can contribute funds into a 401(k). But do keep in mind as of 2016, there is a maximum that can be contributed between employee and employer in the same year. You'll have to stop at $52,000.

WHAT'S A ROTH IRA?

A Roth IRA is an individual retirement account you set up directly with an investment firm. Senator William Roth was the legislative sponsor of the individual retirement account, hence the name Roth IRA.

Here's how they work. When you set up a Roth IRA you work directly with a broker. After you create an account with them, you select the investment options you like, and directly deposit after-tax funds into your Roth IRA.

After you've had the plan for more than five years and are over the age of 59 ½ years old, you can withdraw all of your investment gains and deposits tax free. There are a few exceptions as well. For instance, you can use Roth IRA funds to put a down payment on a home or towards your child's tuition.

Like the 401(k), there are maximum contributions you can make to a Roth IRA. As of 2016 it is $5,500 a year for anyone under the age of fifty. But do keep in mind there are income limits on who can contribute. For instance, if you earn $116,000 individually or $183,000 jointly, you are not allowed to contribute the full amount to a Roth IRA. In some cases you may be excluded from any contributions.

In a sense there is a bit of reverse discrimination going on here. Because if you earn a higher income, you can be phased out of a Roth IRA.

WHAT IS A ROTH 401(k)?

The Roth 401(k) is a new opportunity for many participants. It gives them the ability to use their employer sponsored plan to accumulate after tax dollars for retirement. The allowable amount is significantly higher than the traditional Roth IRA contributions that have been allowed previously. A significant difference in this is that very few plans at this point have adopted this option. Depending upon the age of the participant the Roth 401(k) may make sense for younger people who have more time for the funds to accumulate.

WHAT ARE THE FEATURES OF A 401(k)?

- 401(k) contributions often result in tax savings during the years with contributions

- Many employers offer to match a portion of your contributions

- Contributions can be taken directly out of your paycheck; this is an easy way to contribute without any work on the participant's part. Sort of out of sight, out of mind

- Compared to a Roth IRA, you can contribute more each calendar year with a 401(k)

WHAT ARE THE FEATURES OF A ROTH IRA?

- Since your account is funded with after-tax money, withdrawals are tax-free

- You have the freedom to withdraw your contributions at any time without penalty

- You get to select the brokerage firm and your individual investment options

- You have the freedom to withdraw your contributions at any time without penalty

401(k)	ROTH IRA
Your employer sets up the account	You set up the account with a broker or online platform
Account is funded with pre-tax funds	Account is funded with after-tax funds (from your savings or checking account)
Employer may match your contributions (extra money)	No extra money provided from your employer
Employer selects the plan	You tailor your investments to your needs
Tax penalties for early withdrawal of your contributions	No penalties for early contribution withdrawal (there may be penalties for early earning withdrawal)

WHAT ARE THE FEATURES OF A ROTH 401(k)?

- With a Roth 401(k) the easiest way to describe the features is to use a farm analogy. You pay the taxes on the seed not on the harvest

- Those monies at distribution are tax free

- The rules of the 70 ½ do not apply

- Roth 401(k) can be transferred to beneficiaries tax free

- Ability to contribute more to your Roth 401(k) than was previously allowed with a typical Roth IRA

- You are paying the taxes on the amount that is deposited rather than is distributed

- With automatic deductions it makes participating easy

- Threshold is much higher than what was previously allowed for deposits

It is often the case that union workers have all of their money tied up in retirement accounts where taxes are due at distribution. As an example, I had one client who wanted to pay off his house with money from his retirement account. He didn't realize, until I pointed out, that doing so would put him in a much higher tax bracket.

Knowledge is ultimately power. Having all the facts before you make your final decisions can save you a lot of money. Making sure that there is an element of cohesiveness to your planning can and will make all of the difference in the end.

Whether you're choosing between a 401(k), a Roth IRA, a Roth 401(k), or simply trying to choose which brokerage firm you want to use to make trades and manage your investments, it's important to remember that there is never a one-size-fits-all option. To figure out what is best for you, you have to explore all of the pros and cons with each opportunity and figure out how they relate to your own situation.

The most important thing to remember is that, in most cases, time is on your side. The earlier you start investing and saving for retirement, the better off you will be. So take time to choose which type of retirement options are best for you. But don't let having too many options deter you from making a decision altogether.

THE BASICS OF 401(k) AND ROTH IRA

With most retirement plans including 401(k), Roth 401(k), and Roth IRA there is a 10% penalty from the IRS if you take money out of the plan before the age of 59 ½ .

The other magic number is 70 ½.

At 70 ½ you are required to start taking distributions from 401(k) plans and traditional IRAs. This is the government letting you know that they want their cut, so to speak.

It should be noted that the Roth IRA is tax free at distribution as long as after age 59 ½ and does not have the required minimum distribution rules that apply at age 70 ½.

SHOULD I CONSIDER AN EARLY RETIREMENT PACKAGE?

Story time again. My Uncle John is 53 and was offered a package from the local utility company where he worked. It would cover his health care until a certain age, give him a pension option without penalty, and a lump sum distribution along with a severance package.

At 53 it seemed he was pretty young to retire, but he was curious what his retirement options were. As we formulated the plan, it became obvious that taking the retirement package made the most sense, but the bigger question was, would John re-enter the workforce in a new fashion.

We agreed to pull the retirement lever with the caveat that we would revisit this idea of retirement on a quarterly basis. We would see if John needed to look for other employment. While not all of the stories in this book are good, this one is great. I'm pleased to report that John is now in his late sixties and never did need to re-enter the workforce. Some of this is due to his spending habits but also a result of a well thought through plan, that although has since been modified, has proven itself to work as we always desired.

I have many success stories in my career but this is truly in the top 10, as this was a family member that I could give advice to. Under my team's advice John divested himself from some of the investments that he currently had in his retirement plans. We found they were exposing him to unnecessary risks. The timing turned out to be exceptional as the economy took a turn in a negative direction. I am extremely happy with my team giving this advice to the client, as it saved him from having to put restrictions on his lifestyle.

It might seem like a really easy decision that Uncle John made, but understand that I presented this same scenario to four different individuals, with three of them having stellar retirements. But the fourth did not take my advice and decided to ride it out. I cite Warren Buffett here, who once said, "Be greedy when people are fearful, and fearful when people are greedy." John wasn't greedy, he just wanted a simple retirement and it served him well. Whereas the fourth individual swung for the fences and struck out. This is yet another example of the math being everything. You have to have someone crunch the numbers with you that knows what they are doing. It truly is key to the whole decision making process.

The "buy-out" or early retirement package is becoming increasingly popular with employers. More and more I'm seeing companies offering their workers an early retirement. Why is that? Well, as people gain seniority they become more expensive to the employer. The fact is that younger people just starting out in the work force cost less to employ.

Employers typically offer you a lump-sum distribution based on a few factors; they consider things like age, your years of service, and perhaps most importantly, the finer details in your contract.

Choosing whether or not to accept the terms of an early retirement package is a big deal. It's a major decision. And to say it is a complex choice is an understatement. It's important to not only be informed of the details of the buy-out options, but to also consider your options and your unique circumstances. Before you make the decision to take the money and run, there are some major factors you need to think about. Lucky for you, I've got a few here to get you started.

KEY QUESTION	CONSIDERATION
How will early retirement affect my pension benefits and other retirement income?	- This is data that you can receive from your employer in the offering
Should I start taking Social Security immediately or can I allow my benefits to grow?	- Age is definitely a consideration with this question, along with cash flow and assets available upon retirement.
Does my buy-out come with low or no-cost health insurance until I'm eligible to switch to Medicare?	- This is also data that you can receive from your employer in the offering stage. - If health insurance is excluded from this offering, you should explore the private markets before making a decision.

KEY QUESTION	CONSIDERATION
Have I saved enough for retirement?	- Evaluation of assets accumulated along with income sources available as well as your desired lifestyle in retirement help to answer this question.
What are the tax implications of taking a lump-sum distribution?	- Almost all lump sum distributions are allowed to remain qualified so taxes are paid as the money is paid to the participant rather than at the time it is transferred or rolled over.
How great is the risk of future layoffs from my employer?	- Although no one has a crystal ball, you should have a fair idea of the solvency of your employer. As well, union workers are often laid off by one company only to be hired in short order by another.
Do I love what I do?	- As I mentioned before and will again, we see more and more people retiring from what they have to do to work at what they want to do. If you currently love what you do then keep doing it. Money buys security and freedom but not happiness.

Right about now you may be thinking that is a lot to digest. Let's take a closer look at these one at a time. After all, how do you eat an elephant? Bite by bite.

HOW WILL EARLY RETIREMENT AFFECT MY PENSION BENEFITS AND OTHER RETIREMENT INCOME?

In most instances if your employer would like you to take an early retirement package rather than you wanting to take an early retirement package you may be better off. However there are obviously other circumstances, many of which cannot be planned or that can influence this and the decision on whether to take an early retirement package.

SHOULD I START TAKING SOCIAL SECURITY IMMEDIATELY OR CAN I ALLOW MY BENEFITS TO GROW?

This is usually based on cash flow, lifestyle, and other income sources. Unless a client has a family history of shorter lifespans, then we like to defer social security for at least a few years to maximize the benefits. We utilize a calculator, called the Social Security Analyzer provided through Advisors Excel, that not only tells you the year you should turn on the Social Security tap, but all the way down to the specific month. The other consideration is if you happen to find a job doing something that you really love doing. The income taken from that job may cause this decision to be a no-brainer.

DOES MY BUY-OUT COME WITH LOW OR NO-COST HEALTH INSURANCE UNTIL I'M ELIGIBLE TO SWITCH TO MEDICARE?

This is a huge consideration as health care is one of the primary expenses in retirement. Unfortunately, unless they give you a program along with the details regarding the expenses you will be paying, this is very difficult to predict. I can't tell you how many times this topic alone decided at what point someone was going to retire, and at what time to take an offered retirement package or plan.

HAVE I SAVED ENOUGH FOR RETIREMENT? SHOULD I KEEP WORKING TO BUILD MY NEST EGG?

This is exactly what we cover when we walk through the money map process. We will do the math. We will take all of the contents of your financial junk drawer and make sense of it. We not only want to evaluate the income streams you have like social security, retirement savings, normal savings, assets, and properties, but we also want to look at the tax consequences from each of these income sources.

I can't tell you how many times someone wants to take money out of their retirement plan to pay off their house, until I explain to them that they will be doing so with 65 cents on the dollar. What I mean by that is that if you have one hundred thousand dollars in a retirement account, that income is layered on all of the other income you have for that year, which can force tax payments, and it can move you up more than one tax bracket. This means that you can be paying 35% on every dollar to Uncle Sam.

TAXES. WHAT ARE THE TAX IMPLICATIONS OF TAKING A LUMP-SUM DISTRIBUTION?

The initial implications of taking a lump sum distribution are nil under the assumption that you are moving the monies to an IRA or other qualified plan. Please keep in mind that these dollars are taxed when you actually receive the funds. So if the money hits your bank account, understand that there will be a responsibility to pay the taxes due, either at the time of distribution or when taxes are filed the following year.

This may seem simple but a mistake in this area can be extremely costly. I always advise assistance in this area from someone who does this every day. A misstep here could cost you.

HOW GREAT IS THE RISK OF FUTURE LAYOFFS FROM MY EMPLOYER?

Being laid off is always a risk. The possibility in this new era of automation and technological advances just seems to increase the risk of layoffs. However, you should be able to have a pretty good idea as to your own job security. If not, we can look into the factors that could lead to being laid off by your employer and help you get a better level of comfort in regards to this.

DO I LOVE WHAT I DO FOR A LIVING?

For some, working brings great happiness. If you love what you do, keep at it. That old adage, love what you do and you'll never work a day in your life is very true. So don't feel like you need to retire at a certain age. If you are still able to fulfill your job duties and get some satisfaction from it, then putting retirement off for a while might not be a bad idea.

***

Clearly, there are quite a few factors that weigh-in on the decision to accept or decline a buy-out retirement package. The brief summary we went over is a great tool to start thinking about this major decision. But with the complexities involved, speaking with a retirement investment consultant is a great idea. Once again, I will remind you of how working on the details of retirement in a thoughtful manner helped my Uncle John.

Here's a story to consider. Please keep in mind that as people are living so much longer and living healthier lives, a successful retirement doesn't necessarily need to start at 62 or 65. Let me tell you about Tom. Tom had many options laid out to him for a traditional retirement age, including some incentives for him to leave his employer. We went through the money map process and Tom was going to have no issues to prevent him from sailing off into the sunset of retirement. I caution you to pause, just because everyone thinks you should retire because of age or a particular package, doesn't mean you should.

What everyone is truly trying to accomplish is happiness. And what we found with Tom was that his job was very fulfilling and actually a big part of his identity and self-worth. The idea of Tom getting up each day without having the drive to go to work and continue what he had started seemed much less rewarding to him than the path of retirement. So Tom, even though in his late sixties, is still working today. For him, this is his best and most purposeful retirement.

So be careful of what influences you on making this decision. Regardless of what an advisor or family member might say, you must make this decision for yourself. Remember, once you take that package the rules all change.

SHOULD I CONSIDER A BUY-OUT RETIREMENT PACKAGE?

Is your employer offering you a buy-out package or are you seeking one?

What would you do if you retired early? Would it bring you greater happiness?

How would a buy-out package affect your overall retirement plan?

HOW DOES SOCIAL SECURITY WORK?

When you were a kid, you probably had a piggy bank. When people gave you some change, you'd feed the piggy. One day, you decided that you needed that money, so out came your father's hammer and little piggy was busted open. At that moment, when you tallied up your money you were probably either excited or disappointed.

With Social Security, you essentially are putting away money into a piggy bank, money you'll want later on. But many factors will decide if you are excited or disappointed when you "bust" your Social Security open to see what's inside. If you work to your full age you might receive a benefit of $2,400 at age 70. But you may only receive $1,600 if you take it at age 62. So you can see there are consequences when you break into Social Security early.

One situation that I get a lot is the I'm going to take it now while the getting is good scenario. People are always talking about getting their money out before Social Security doesn't exist anymore. The truth is that the largest demographic of the population is currently millennials rather than baby boomers. With Social Security there are a lot of opinions on what the future of is going to be like or whether it will even exist at all. My opinion is that I plan for what exists and will adapt to changes as required.

WHAT ARE THE BASICS OF SOCIAL SECURITY?

At the basic level Social Security does two main things. It collects and distributes funds. If you work in the United States, you pay taxes into Social Security. Social Security takes that tax money and pays out benefits to those who are eligible.

Depending upon your age, you could draw out of Social Security as early as 62. At 66 you've reached what is considered your full retirement age, but you can increase your income further by deferring up to age 70. Up until your full retirement age of 66, you are restricted in the amount of income you are allowed to earn. At ages 62 to age 66 you can earn just under $16,000, then every two dollars you earn above that level reduces your Social Security by one dollar.

WHO'S ELIGIBLE FOR SOCIAL SECURITY?

Believe it or not Social Security is not just for retirees. Depending on your circumstances, you can be eligible to receive benefits at any age. How is that? There are four types of people who are eligible to receive Social Security benefits:

- Folks who've already retired;

- People who are disabled;

- The survivors of workers who've passed away; and

- The dependents of beneficiaries.

WHEN AM I ELIGIBLE TO RECEIVE MY FULL BENEFITS?

Unfortunately, there isn't a simple answer. But it's not as confusing as it seems. As of 2017, if you were born between 1943 and 1960, your full retirement benefits age increases incrementally up to age 67. For fast reference, if you were born in 1950 or earlier, you are in luck. You're already eligible for your full Social Security benefit. Below is a chart, taken from the Social Security website, to help you discover your full retirement age.

BIRTH YEAR	FULL RETIREMENT AGE
1943-1954	66
1955	66 and 2 months
1956	66 and 4 months
1957	66 and 6 months
1958	66 and 8 months
1959	66 and 10 months
1960 or later	67

WHAT HAPPENS IF I RETIRE EARLY?

Basically you can start to collect benefits at age 62. However the Social Security Administration will reduce those benefits if you start early to the tune of one-half of one percent for each month you begin collecting benefits prior to your full retirement age. Should your full retirement age be 66 and two months, and you start collecting Social Security when you're 62, then you would receive just 74.2 percent of your potential full retirement benefits.

WHAT IF I DELAY MY RETIREMENT?

Delaying when you start to receive your benefits past your full retirement age amounts to Social Security increasing your benefits by a certain percentage amount in relation to your birth year.

WHAT DO I DO TO APPLY FOR SOCIAL SECURITY BENEFITS?

When you are ready to apply for your benefits from Social Security you can do so at their website: socialsecurity.gov/applyforbenefits.

You should plan to do this several months in advance of when you would want your benefits to begin. They may ask for certain paperwork such as your Social Security card, birth certificate, proof of U.S. citizenship or lawful immigration status, marriage certificate, your spouse's information, any military discharge papers, and your most recent tax return.

EXTRA THOUGHTS ABOUT SOCIAL SECURITY

- People have been thinking that the program would disappear for a long time. It hasn't and probably won't. Either way, you shouldn't make decisions based on fears. Someone who does this may find themselves shortchanged.

- There are now more millennials than baby boomers, which should predict that the program will continue.

- If you are a widow you can receive Social Security (also known as survivor's benefits) at age 60.

- If you earn income from wages or other sources you could end up paying up to 85% taxes on your Social Security benefits.

Of course this is a crude and rudimentary overview of some of the aspects of Social Security benefits. The truth is, Social Security benefits can be extremely confusing and complicated. And just when you think you have a handle on things, some of the rules, exceptions, and exclusions are subject to change. It's a financial planner's job to know all the details and wrinkles involved with Social Security benefits. If you have any pressing questions about Social Security and how it impacts your retirement plans, reach out to a financial consultant.

THE BASICS OF SOCIAL SECURITY

- Age based as to when you can begin receiving benefits

- Each year (until age 70) that you put off receiving benefits, your monthly amount goes up

- The amount you receive is based upon your lifelong income and the amount you paid in

- There is a maximum benefit amount

- Spousal income option with special provisions for widows and widowers

- There are cost of living increases but no guarantees on them

- You can earn some income while receiving Social Security benefits without penalty

AFFORDING HEALTH CARE IN RETIREMENT

Without good health, an integral part to a great quality of life, you have little else. Ask any dying billionaire and they'll probably give their last cent for a cure to whatever ails them. Have a heartfelt conversation with someone who has lost a spouse to illness and to be sure, they'd have begged, borrowed, or stolen if it meant more time with the one they loved. In the end it is always about health and being healthy enough to enjoy life.

A friend of mine and sufferer from smart-guy-itis told me about the English philosopher John Locke, who controversially published in an essay the idea that people were entitled to natural and fundamental rights. In short these rights were life, liberty, and the pursuit of property. Think about that. Out of all the things of this earth he could select, he picked just those three. But more than that, in this highly curated list, he put life first. It would seem for John Locke, of all things, life was of the highest importance. I'm sure that when you stop to think about what truly matters, you would agree with Mr. Locke. After all, without life, not a bit of the rest of it matters.

Ever consider this common toast: "To your health!" Or how about, "Salud!" Translated into English, it simply means health. In Arab countries, it isn't uncommon to say, "Sahtein," literally meaning "two healths," before beginning a meal. But we don't have to travel far, to explicitly see the importance of health. Look no further than the continued division politically in America in regards to how to handle health care. Health, life, and vitality is clearly an important and integral aspect of our society.

We all know the importance of health and how important it is to stay in good health. But as we age, and probably grow wiser about the subject, placing a higher value on it, we are suddenly hit with the realities of the situation. Most of us will need medical care. Most of us will have prescription medications that we will come to depend upon. We will need to see doctors and even specialists from time to time. Some of us will need even more still. Some of us will need operations, in-home health aides, and even long-term nursing care facilities at some point. And here is the thing about all of that, we will have to have a means to pay for it.

One of the primary things to consider in retirement is how to afford health care costs after your career has come to an end. If you haven't been living in a cave this whole time, then you are probably aware of the exponential rate at which health care costs rise. When you couple that staggeringly steady cost growth with the continued increase of life expectancy, it is difficult to pin down just how much you need to save in order to match the price of health care as you age.

In my career I've seen just about every possible scenario play out. Even still, new ones seem to pop-up on a daily basis. The only constant is that you have to be prepared for the unexpected. Because if you are not prepared, then you remove what little control you might have had from the equation.

As an example, and I could cite you many, my father-in-law owned a concrete business for most of his life. Recently he stepped away and sold it to my brother-in-law. And although I'm slightly offended it wasn't offered to me, the point of the story remains the same. Even though he has since retired, my mother-in-law is still employed and will remain so until she turns 65, purely for the purpose of maintaining health insurance. This is a far more common situation and often times the number one consideration when choosing a retirement date. Besides having to be knowledgeable about certain factors such as COBRA and the age at which Medicare kicks in, there are lots of other elements that need to be kept on your radar, no matter where in the arc of retirement planning you currently are. Obviously, owning a concrete business is different from being a medical professional, but the problematic issues that they faced can confront a person in any profession.

Think about this. Many Americans over the age of 50 haven't set aside funds for their out-of-pocket medical expenses. You might be in this category. Considering that we are now regularly living past age 80, and that the amount of time we are retired is longer, and that new cutting edge medical advances are more expensive than ever, how is it that we aren't spending more time considering squirreling away funds for health care? This is concerning!

So, in the spirit of John Locke, I've come up with three keys to consider for that all important question about your health: how will I pay for health care in retirement? If this one subject seems complicated, it's because it is. Truthfully, it is extremely so. In fact, we have a full-time person focused on this specific area because of its complexities.

Don't let it raise your blood pressure though. I promise that with a well-executed plan, you'll end up more worried about which golf club to use on that par four approach shot, rather than about how to pay for your health care costs. Let's try and break it down so that it is easily digested. Here we go:

QUESTION	CONSIDERATION
What are my health care needs?	Individual factors like age, health, family medical history can drastically change potential expenses. Even your list of current or potential medications is a consideration when choosing a plan.
Am I eligible for any employer sponsored health care programs?	Employee benefits you receive can help offset costs and positively alter the amount you need to save for medical expenses. Learning your program options or finding a trusted advisor in this area is a must if you hope to truly take advantage of and learn the intricacies of your health care plan and options.

How much will Medicare cover?	For most retirees, Medicare is the backbone of their health care plan. But like most things over time, Medicare has gone through significant changes. There are also many supplements available to run alongside of the Medicare plan. These can prove beneficial.

You know the drill. Let's take a closer look at these three key questions.

WHAT ARE MY HEALTH CARE NEEDS?

This is where you would look specifically at your individual and situational factors such as family longevity, your current health, and your health care options. Then you have to ask yourself, and try to answer honestly, do you get sick often? Do you go to the doctor's office frequently? How about urgent care facilities? What would you do if you had to go to the emergency room? Some of you will have a good handle on what to expect in regards to your future health care needs, but others won't. And the truth is that none of us have a crystal ball. We have to remember that bad things happen, most times without warning. But again, having a plan in place to deal with the unexpected as well as the expected, will almost always make a bad situation a little easier to handle for both you and your loved ones.

AM I ELIGIBLE FOR ANY EMPLOYER SPONSORED HEALTH CARE PROGRAMS?

It's important to speak with a financial consultant to comb over the details of your plan. The better you understand and utilize the benefits your employer has given you, the lower your total health care costs will be. Knowing specifically what your employer plan allows, and what it looks like when you retire, is extremely important. You absolutely want to have a handle on what your maximum out-of-pocket expenses could be. Of course I say this knowing that you cannot accurately project what you will spend on unforeseen medical costs. But you may have a good idea based on your historic needs and their costs. When looking at the details of the plan options this needs to be looked at very closely, because you may be stuck with what you pick for at least a year, even though you have the option to change plans on your anniversary date.

HOW MUCH WILL MEDICARE COVER?

Traditionally, Medicare Parts A and B provide coverage for most needed medical visits at both the doctor's office and the hospital. You can reasonably figure on Medicare Parts A and B to cover 80% of the cost. The remaining 20% of the costs will need to be paid either as an out of pocket expense or through the use of Medicare supplements. Be fully aware though, this is not a hard and fast rule. In order for your Medicare to cover the 80% the billed item must qualify as an allowable charge. As an example, elective procedures such as cosmetic surgery typically would not qualify as an allowable charge covered by Medicare. You can find a list of procedures and medications not covered at medicare.gov, as well consulting your financial consultant's health care experts. They're always happy to assist you with this.

MEDICARE SUPPLEMENTS

Medicare supplements are used by many to cover or reduce the 20% of the costs not covered by Medicare alone. These Medicare supplements, or Medigap plans as they are also known, should be discussed with your financial consultant's health care coverage expert as there are many options to choose from. Not all of these options may best suit your specific needs.

WHAT WILL MEDICARE NOT COVER?

Much of your traditional hospitalization may be covered by Medicare, but as you age and need non-traditional care situations (such as an in-home health aide, a nursing home, or even hospice), you might find that those treatment options may not be covered by, or at least covered much less than expected. If you are reliant on a government program to cover your needs, you will have less in the way of options and of course that could make you unhappy. If you are left in a situation without much assets, most of the higher-end care facilities will have little interest in taking care of you as they prefer a traditional premium paying resident. Also, we have seen many folks not even have the option to be in an area that is familiar to them, such as where they have grown up, or grown old, or located near family. It is often the case that someone without options or assets is relocated to a facility based on space, not location.

WHAT ALTERNATIVE MEASURES EXIST?

The short answer is that there are two fairly common, but not that well-known, alternative measures. The first is traditional long-term care insurance. This is insurance that is extremely costly because of the risk that the insurance company takes on. With 50% of us needing some kind of long-term care in our lives, and depending on the amount of time that the insurance company could potentially be on the hook, as well as the rising costs of health care in general, it is no wonder that this option isn't the most cost effective.

Traditional long-term care insurance used to be much more popular than it is now. This is because of the prohibitive costs associated with this plan. As well, another big drawback to this type of insurance is that when you die, all of the premiums are simply kept by the insurance company. It's true that you have the opportunity to buy a rider that will pass your lifetime premiums on to your heirs, but adding this feature is usually very costly. That is why most people decline this option.

The second alternative measure, which is far more typical, is the use of the newest version of life insurance. We will likely discuss this product more than once in this book because it is a tool that is like the Swiss army knife of insurance. The newest versions of Indexed Universal Life have a hybrid option that allows, in some cases, a person that is in need of long-term care or has a chronic illness to take a portion of the death benefit while they are still alive, to use for such care. This is an option that people have but are not required to execute or use at all. Most people are not familiar with this option but we believe that it has merits.

So now that we've covered that, let's reflect on the fact that after life, John Locke listed liberty. In addition to the basic health costs, it's also important to think about how you will remain independent as you age. How will you remain independent if you should one day require some assistance with daily living?

In 2016 Genworth conducted a cost of care study, in part, to better determine the financial cost of a part-time home health aide. What did they find out? Nationwide the median cost for home health aide services is upward of $125 a day. You don't need to be a math prodigy to figure how fast $875 bucks a week adds up. Costs can be even scarier for full time services like nursing home care. These are major expenditures that Medicare and employer sponsored insurance typically don't fully cover.

To help in the illustration of these points, let me tell you a story that is personal to me. You see I grew up in Pemberville, Ohio in a 900-square-foot ranch home. My Dad was a welder and my Mother worked for the church and at other jobs. We were part of a hard-working family as a whole. The patriarch of my family was my Grandfather on my Father's side. He owned and operated a towing service, so it was not uncommon for us to be at their home and watch as he had to speed off to pull someone out of a ditch. This was indeed more than just a job. It was a way of life for the DeVerna family.

The junk yard, or the "yard" as well called it, was like a Starbucks of today. The yard was where many of the local personalities would check in with my Grandfather, Dolas, and the boys. In addition, my Dad had his weld shop there and my

Uncle and Cousin both worked at the yard. Now fast forward to when my grandfather became ill and passed away. At first my grandmother moved in with us, but in no time at all her health deteriorated, in part due to losing her spouse of 65 years, as well as the general wear and tear on her body from a lifetime of working. Before long my parents could no longer care for her at our house.

She ended up having to go into a long-term care facility. The part that always gets me is that in no time at all their house and the yard, they places they had worked their whole lives for, had to be sold to pay for her care. This in turn had a negative impact on my uncle and cousin as well as my father. They all worked there too.

Quickly all of what I had known to represent my family's hard work and community building efforts was gone, sold to the highest bidder. Nowadays, it only exists as a distant memory to a few of us.

Had there been any type of preparation or planning, this could have been avoided. So it breaks my heart that I wasn't in this line of work at the time. Maybe then, my grandfather's legacy could have been saved in some more fortunate capacity.

So in a world where they are telling us that half of us are needing this type of care and I think it's going to be you and you think it's going to be me, it is best to cover your bases and take care of your family and your stuff. Because no one cares more about your stuff then you do.

This is your one and only life. For your health, please start saving. Or better yet, schedule a meeting with your financial guy today. Salud!

HOW DO I PLAN FOR HEALTH CARE IN RETIREMENT?

Know what you are offered through employer-sponsored plans

Know what you are offered through government programs

Pay attention to the details of medical maintenance and prescriptions drug costs

Know your maximum out-of-pocket costs for a year

Weigh out best and worst case scenarios annually for the programs offered

Pay close attention to looming deadlines

LONG-TERM CARE ISSUES AND LIFE INSURANCE

If you fail to plan, you're planning to fail. This famous wit is attributed to founding father, Benjamin Franklin. If you've spent any time in an office, there's a solid chance you've seen this quote on a motivational poster or two. But it's much more than just a quaint, glib little saying.

When we look deeper into this line there are two things that strike me. First, failing is easy. You don't have to do anything to fail. It's a default mode. And second, is the opposite. Success is something that must be planned for. You have to execute on your prepared plan to fight off failure and achieve success.

If you remember Aesop's fable about the ant and the grasshopper than you will remember that the ant toiled all summer long preparing for winter while the grasshopper did not. Then when winter rolled around, the grasshopper came to the ant in desperate need. The point of the story is that those who prepare for life's winter will succeed in staving off hard times while those who choose to ignore the future's needs will fail. The same logic can certainly be applied to long-term care and life insurance.

While we tend to apply these truths to finance and preparing for natural disasters or unforeseen circumstances, I'd like for us to think about planning for health. It's something we don't like to think about. We'd like to think we'd live forever in perfect health. But for most people reading this book, you have probably already been exposed to the realities of health issues that everyone can have occur in their lifetime. For many of you as well, you have lost loved ones unexpectedly. Perhaps you have even seen the consequences of death from the standpoint of costs associated with funeral arrangements and estate issues. But if we bury our heads in the sand and ignore planning for the future, we are guaranteeing failure. So let's take a moment to look at long-term health care and life insurance as you eye your retirement.

WHAT ARE LONG-TERM CARE ISSUES?

Insurance companies look at a certain set of criteria called Activities of Daily Living when evaluating whether you qualify for actually using the policy. A doctor must be willing to say that you need assistance with at least two of these things:

Bathing: Getting into the tub or shower

Dressing: Putting on any necessary clothing including undergarments and necessary braces, fasteners, or artificial limbs

Transferring: Getting into a bed, chair, or wheelchair and getting back out

Toilet: Getting to and from the toilet, getting on and off the toilet, and performing personal hygiene

Continence: Maintaining control of bowel and bladder function; or when unable, performing necessary associated hygiene such as catheterization

Eating: Feeding yourself by getting food into your mouth from a plate or cup and being able to use utensils. When unable to feed yourself from a container, being able to feed yourself using a feeding tube

SOME SIMPLE TRUTHS TO CONSIDER ABOUT THE THREE WAYS TO PAY FOR LONG-TERM CARE:

1. **Private Pay:** This is where you write the check every month out of your bank account. This scenario only works if you have the means to facilitate it for an indefinite period of time.

2. **Long-Term Care Insurance:** This is a great planning tool but requires both foresight and money. These types of plans can be very costly because the insurance company faces a great deal of exposure financially as long-term care is expensive in general. Another issue to consider when buying long-term care

is that if it goes unused the monies that you paid in premiums essentially disappear.

3. **Life Insurance with a Long-Term Care Rider:** With these types of hybrid policies at the very least your family will get the death benefit if the long-term care benefits go unused, essentially hedging your bet. These types of policies are generally less expensive because they are based on mortality rather than morbidity. As well they have a pre-determined cap as to the amount that the insurance company is potentially on the hook for.

4. **Government Assistance:** If you do not have either the means to comfortably pay for long-term care of either your spouse or you or both and do not hold either a long-term care insurance policy or a life insurance policy with a long-term care rider then the government restricts the amount of assets you are allowed to keep and the amount of income you are allowed to make, forcing a "spend down" scenario.

POSSIBLE FAILURES	PLANNING OPTIONS
Not enough money	Less affected by a forced "spend down" and likely less lifestyle change.

POSSIBLE FAILURES	PLANNING OPTIONS
Money but no insurance	Have resources to spend for long-term care.
No significant money but good planning with the use trusts, use of insurances, etc.	Ability to leverage money to your advantage through planning of techniques.

DO I REALLY NEED LIFE INSURANCE?

You've heard this from me before, but people only get life insurance for one of two reasons, either they owe somebody or they love somebody. Let's assume you meet one of those criteria and take quick look at life insurance options.

TERM LIFE INSURANCE

With the different basic types of Term Life Insurance you: (a) buy a policy for a certain period of time, or (b) buy it up to a certain age, or (c) have the policy as long as you work for a certain employer. The benefits are that this type of policy is inexpensive, but you are likely to outlive the policy.

WHOLE LIFE INSURANCE

Whole Life Insurance is a permanent type of life insurance with a cash value element to it. The cash value inside of the policy is tied in closely with interest rates. This was one of the original forms of life insurance, but has underperformed due to record low interest rates. Typically a person bought

Whole Life Insurance in the 70s or 80s when interest rates were high. They were told that not only would it act as a life insurance policy but it could serve as a retirement plan. Now those same people are upset because their policies have underperformed.

UNIVERSAL LIFE INSURANCE

Universal Life is insurance with a cash value to it. The cash value inside the policy is tied closely to the investment performance of the insurance company. These policies, although they are not performing above or even at expectations, have far exceeded the performance of Whole Life contracts.

INDEXED UNIVERSAL LIFE INSURANCE

This is another cash value life insurance policy, with this kind of life insurance, the insurance company uses an indexed account tied to different indices such as the S&P 500. The insurance company buys options which then allows them to capture a greater upside in positive market years while still being capped on the downside based on contractual guarantees.

With the Whole, Universal, and Indexed Universal varieties there exists both a ceiling and a floor that is guaranteed by contractual obligation.

VARIABLE UNIVERSAL LIFE INSURANCE

Yet another cash value life insurance policy, but rather than the investments being chosen by the insurance company, they are selected by the policy owner. These investments look much more like something you might see in your 401(k), with the possibility of being somewhat aggressive if desired. The biggest problem with these policies is the management of volatility.

If nothing else, life insurance offers protection for you and your loved ones. Life insurance is not always the best financial investment, but knowing that your loved will be okay financially, should something happen to you, is worth a great deal.

Knowing which type of life insurance plan is best for you and your family is not something that I would expect to come naturally to you. I have been helping people with their life insurance needs for a long time and stand ready to help you navigate these confusing waters. Remember, it is your money and you are the captain of the ship, but I can be your trusted navigator and pilot.

PASSING ON LIFE INSURANCE	PASSING WITH LIFE INSURANCE
CON - Exposure to estate taxes	PRO - Tax-free income distributed to beneficiaries
CON - Family exposed to debts	PRO - Benefit paid outside of probate
CON - Family exposed to lost income	PRO - Cash is provided to cover estate taxes or other debts

Sometimes decisions have to be made about circumstances that are uncomfortable. Nobody enjoys thinking about long-term care and ultimately death. These uncomfortable subjects should never be ignored. But there are ways to approach them without causing undue stress. I've always found that talking about them and planning for them well in advance from the neutral ground of your financial guy's office makes dealing with these things a lot easier for everyone. So schedule an appointment today and you can leave with knowing you have a plan in place rather than always having an uncomfortable reality lingering in the back of your head.

LONG-TERM CARE & LIFE INSURANCE

Many forms of life insurance now have a living benefit that can be accessed prior to death if certain qualifications are met

If used correctly the cash value inside of a life insurance policy can be accessed on a tax-free basis even if you have no intentions of repayment

With the increased mortality rates in people living longer than ever the cost of insurance has never been lower

With the recent living benefits being added to certain types of life insurance the access to cash for alternative purposes such as long-term care, has become a bit of a Swiss Army knife

HOW CAN A FINANCIAL CONSULTANT HELP ME RETIRE?

Many of you have had the gift of children. And you probably remember the time when you were nervously getting everything ready for the coming baby. You turned a bedroom into a nursery. You assembled a crib. You baby-proofed the house the best you could. You set up a rocking chair in the corner and put the changing table by the window. You did the research on which swaddling blankets were the best, which bedding was the safest for your new baby. You even packed a bag in advance for when that big moment would arrive. You left nothing to chance. You sought out advice from your parents and other people. Maybe even read books by experts. The point is that you prepared yourself with everything from knowledge to the implementation of a well thought out plan.

Then one day, anticipated but somehow unexpectedly, the time has come. You're going to bring your baby into the world. When it's your first child, you're certain to get lots of advice. But somehow that all goes out the window when the moment is here. And you find yourself relying on the aid and help of the nursing staff, the midwives, and the doctors. In that moment, you find yourself relying on their expertise. You've never done this before. All the experiences, pains, and pitfalls are new to you. But for the nurses and doctors, it's another Tuesday at the office. They have loads of experience. They know the tips and strategies to help you with the biggest day of your life.

The same goes for your retirement. Odds are, you have never planned for your retirement before. It's a big day. Sure you've probably gotten some advice from those who've gone through it before, but for a financial consultant who focuses on retirement planning, they have the strategies, tips, and advice you can count on to make sure your dreams are fully realized.

Before we push ahead and end the labor, let's take a moment to breath. Let's look at a few ways a financial consultant can help you retire.

SYMPTOM	DIAGNOSIS
Do you have a retirement strategy?	- A financial consultant can help you maximize income while managing your risk
Do you have experienced guidance?	- Financial consultants (focusing on retirement) help people retire every day - We offer a range of tested and proven services that help you reach your goals

Are you protected from the unknown?	- With experience and guidance, you can be prepared for unseen hurdles
	- We can help you setup a legacy for your family

WHAT FINANCIAL GUIDANCE HAVE YOU HAD UP UNTIL NOW?

For many people an experience like this might seem familiar. You've had someone managing your 401(k) and/or other assets. Maybe you speak to them often or maybe you've left the heavy lifting of decision making up to them. Perhaps you have only met for donuts and coffee on the odd occasion with no real advice given.

Yet for others of you, perhaps you are the do-it-yourself types, and have grabbed the bull by the horns and managed everything all alone. No matter what your experience with financial guidance has been, the reality is this. As retirement nears, the gravity of the situation becomes much more significant.

People in their younger years are typically more worried about outperforming the market. But as you get to the retirement stage, the rate of return takes on less importance. It's the quality of the overall plan that becomes paramount. Not many people feel comfortable pulling the retirement lever without the knowledge that the ever important math has truly been done.

Although I have met some people capable of crunching these numbers, my recommendation is always to meet with someone who focuses on this type of financial planning and does it as their primary occupation. Frankly, there are a lot of moving parts to grapple with.

WHAT'S MY RETIREMENT STRATEGY?

I can't stress enough the importance of a good retirement plan. This is the rest of your life. Why would you just wing it? Financial consultants can look at your unique needs and situation, and develop a strategy and plan that is tailored to you.

Whether you consider yourself an aggressive or a conservative investor, it is always advisable to have a great strategy. Unless you're in the upper stratosphere of wealth, you are going to need a plan to adhere to. For most of us, we fall in a category closer to the middle of the spectrum where our needs are not completely met by the state and likewise we are not so well off that we can do whatever we want without financial consequences.

Good planning can mean the difference between an uncertain fate or one where choices are positive in nature and we are the ones choosing them. Obviously, there are always situations that can arise beyond our control. But don't let these fears prevent you from formulating a sound plan for your retirement.

WHAT KIND OF GUIDANCE DO I HAVE FOR RETIREMENT?

Let me give you an example. A client walked in after having used an online tool to determine his options and his best way forward. The problem was that he had made some mistakes and some poor assumptions.

For one, he used a number for his rate of return on his investments that didn't calculate accurately the whole story of the market's performance. For example, when the market was down, way down in 07 and 08, it had a major effect on the overall strength of a portfolio overtime.

Now as much as we would all like to pretend like that crisis never took place, it did. If you don't figure in occurrences like that into your plan, you'll be making the same kinds of poor assumptions that this gentlemen made. My advice is always to plan thoroughly, to be honest in your planning, and to seek help from someone who deals with these types of things every day.

But it doesn't end there. This same client made other poor assumptions when working with the online tool. He assumed that he knew when and how often he would need a new vehicle, and even scarier, he thought that he could predict when he would need long-term care. I assure you that had he been able to correctly predict this, I would have hired him on the spot!

Another caution to think about when using online software tools, is that they usually don't have inflation factored in, or any guidance on Social Security and what year that should be turned on, and almost never will you see a pension calculator.

AM I PROTECTED FROM THE UNKNOWN?

One of the unique parts of working with someone who does this every day is that they see things that you could not possibly even know to look for. When it comes to retirement planning the real pitfall (which will seem painfully obvious once I've said it) is that you don't want to be in a position where running out of money is possible.

When you work with someone who focuses on retirement planning, rather than someone whose endeavor is to maximize the biggest possible ROI, differences in strategy go hand in hand with the fact that the end goals are not the same. Likewise, in this modern world you can find advice on how to do everything with a Google search or by watching a two minute YouTube video. But you wouldn't necessarily set out to climb Mt. Everest after watching an instructional video some guy made in his basement, would you? Well let's hope that you put that same sort of weight in the decision making when it comes to the guide who will get you safely to the summit of your retirement.

I mean that one way or another you are paying for the guidance, so make sure that your guide has the same goals in mind as you. More importantly, be certain that your guide fully realizes what your goals really are. It is all too easy to get swept up in risky plays. But remember this. It is the sexy maneuvers that often help you cross the finish line.

There is an immense amount of importance when preparing for the unexpected pitfalls of life. An experienced financial consultant, especially one focused on retirement planning, can help you be best prepared to conquer what lies ahead.

While it may be uncomfortable to address, it's crucial to ensure our loved ones and family are taken care of in our absence. A financial consultant can help you set up a legacy for your family.

I have had experience with people failing to change their beneficiaries, leaving their estates to the wrong person. In today's world, second and third marriages are common place. An atmosphere of his, hers, and theirs kind of thinking exists. This can complicate things. And in my experience it becomes less of an issue if addressed by a financial consultant in a professional atmosphere rather than being tackled at the breakfast table.

In the world we live in these days, it is very common for couples to have children from previous relationships. This can complicate matters and become very uncomfortable. Worse still, is that if these types of issues are not planned for in advance, the loved ones left behind can have real problems. Planning for all of these types of issues with a financial consultant can save a lot of unnecessary trouble.

So just like you sought advice from doctors, nurses, midwives, mom, and probably a lot of books before you brought your baby home, the same logic should be applied to bringing the baby of your retirement plan home. And just like how you didn't do the first life experience all alone, you don't want to try to plan for such an important milestone in life alone.

Don't worry. You don't have to think about your retirement alone. My team and I are here to guide you every step of the way. We are here for all those hard decisions, the uncomfortable moments, the dreaming, the planning, the execution, and the point at which you pull that proverbial lever and cross the finish line. We'll even be here to help you beyond that moment. I promise that no matter what, we'll make the process as easy and rewarding as possible so that you can have the potential to live your dream retirement to its maximum capacity.

HOW CAN A FINANCIAL CONSULTANT HELP ME RETIRE?

With a financial consultant you will have access to an array of specialized tools like:

+ Social Security calculator

+ Pension plan calculator

+ Risk analysis software

+ Money map program

+ Legacy plan generation

+ A whole team of professionals devoted to the success of your retirement!

RETIREMENT IS JUST THE BEGINNING

Wow! This is fantastic. You made it to the end of this book. Pat yourself on the back. You do have endurance. I know that there were probably times while reading this that you wanted to give up. There were probably chapters that seemed incredibly boring and some that were even uncomfortable. But you persevered anyway. I've got to tell you, I'm proud of you. I know that it wasn't easy to get through all of this. But look, you've come this far, and the best part is that retirement is just the beginning.

No, I'm not going to make you read more chapters on 401(k) or long-term care. But I do want to say that you have no excuses now not to grab the bull by the horns and take charge of your future.

So now that you're ready to get serious about your retirement, throw the keys to me. I'll help get you there safely. I promise. That is after all what I do, day in and day out. I help people navigate the tough stuff, the boring bits, and the exciting parts, where your dream retirement is just waiting to become a reality.

Throughout this book we've talked about the importance of the retirement red zone, as well as fun stuff like what your dream retirement could look like. Remember that RV resort in Florida? Or how about the exciting possibilities of retiring to a new location, maybe even one overseas, where sunscreen and what colorful drink to order next are your biggest worries? We delved into a lot of how's and why's and technical things that may have helped you fall asleep while reading those chapters.

And sure we did the uncomfortable. We went over things like the possibility of needing long-term care, the costs of health care, and even how to secure protection in the event of death. I know that it wasn't the most fun to discuss these things, but it's always better not to get caught with your pants down, so we did discuss them. And you survived. You're better off and smarter for having taken the time to learn about these issues.

But I want to return to the title of this chapter. Retirement is just the beginning. What does that mean? Well, simply put, the end of this book, is just the beginning of your next chapter. It's the beginning of your journey to constructing your dream retirement.

Now comes the part where we put the plan together. As we do so, we'll tackle the tough stuff, we'll crunch the numbers. We'll explore your dreams and do our best to make them a reality. As we do this together, you will acquire protection, confidence, and all of the tools to set sail into the best years of your life. The years where you are rewarded for all of your hard work and service.

For each of you, your dream retirements will be uniquely yours. They may involve spending more time with loved ones, or road tripping across the country in an RV, or riding into the sunset on that motorcycle you've always had your eye on. Maybe you'll finally make the move to your favorite spot by the sea, where the fish are always biting and the sun is always shining. Then again, maybe retiring from your job, is just so that you can pursue your next career. Maybe you finally get the chance to start that small business you've been thinking about for years now.

Whatever the case, with the right plan in place, and with the help of your ship's navigator and pilot we'll get you there. I can't promise smooth sailing all the way. But I can promise that if done right, you'll have all the tools to make it around the horn.

So collect your financial junk drawer and come and dump it on my desk. The sooner the better. Because retirement is just the beginning!